W9-BEX-479

The Stamp Bug

The Stamp Bug

An Illustrated Introduction to Stamp Collecting

Douglas and Mary Patrick

McGRAW-HILL RYERSON LIMITED
Toronto   Montreal   New York   St. Louis   San Francisco
Auckland   Beirut   Bogotá   Düsseldorf   Johannesburg
Lisbon   London   Lucerne   Madrid   Mexico   New Delhi
Panama   Paris   San Juan   São Paulo   Singapore
Sydney   Tokyo

The Stamp Bug

ISBN 0-07-082779-6

1 2 3 4 5 6 7 8 9 10   THB   7 6 5 4 3 2 1 0 9 8

Printed and bound in Canada

Canadian Cataloguing in Publication Data

Patrick, Douglas, date
    The stamp bug

ISBN 0-07-082779-6

1. Postage-stamps — Collectors and collecting.
I. Patrick, Mary, date. II. Title.

HE6213.P38   769.56'023   C78-001477-4

Acknowledgments

The authors are grateful for the editorial help of Thomas C. Fairley, book editor, Gordon Froggatt, newspaper editor, Jim F. Webb, Canadian Stamp Dealer, and George S. Wegg, professional philatelist.

Patricia Daly created the mythical character called "The Stamp Bug," and unintentionally opened the way for other artists and photographers to illustrate this book: J. Allan Moffatt photographed the stamps in the glossary; Ernie Lawson illustrated five different kinds of papers used for printing stamps and also enlarged a small list from Scott's Postage Stamp Catalogue, Volume One. Harold Robinson photographed the children, the accessories, stamps for identifying the countries of origin, and everything else in the book.

Representation of the cartoon character "STAMP BUG" is copyright and has been registered in Canada by Douglas and Mary Patrick. Applications have been made in the United States.

CONTENTS

FOREWORD

Once more Douglas and Mary Patrick have done it. They have produced a book entitled, "The Stamp Bug," which is written for the young collector and the layman in stamps.

Their past history is such that they will go down in the annals of Canadian philately as a couple who have constantly performed a service for their fellow collector. The book that they have written is enjoyable, clear, and concise and is useful for any collector worldwide. We will always be indebted to Doug and Mary for helping to get the beginner stamp collector on the road to being a philatelist.

John H.M. Young
Chairman, Editorial Board
British North American Philatelic Society

To Sherri Lee-Anne
and
Andrew John Patrick

INTRODUCTION

The Stamp Bug is an odd little fellow. He does not live in a body like some other bugs and insects, but comes along to fascinate boys and girls, men and women alike. He is a feeling, a sensation or desire that strikes young and old. Be proud when some person says, "You've got the Stamp Bug." Thousands of the best-known people in the world also got the Stamp Bug at some time in their lives.

People in a wide variety of occupations collect postage stamps, for example Alain de Cadenet the famous British racing car driver. He knows so much about British King George V stamps that Stanley Gibbons the catalogue publishers hired him to rewrite that section in the 1978 specialized catalogue.

In Toronto during the stamp exhibition named CAPEX — June 9 to 18, 1978 — Mr. de Cadenet said, "I'll enjoy showing America that you don't have to be conventional to be a stamp collector." He finished his conversation saying, "Stamp collecting is a wonderful therapy — lots of people agree — even Sir Gordon Richards, a jockey for Queen Elizabeth; he collects postage stamps."

Bobby Moore, a British football player is another stamp collector, Mr. Cadenet explained and added, "I was managing Graham Hill's automobile racing team some years ago when he opened STAMPEX the annual British stamp show. He nearly fell to the floor when he saw I had won a gold medal."

In the United States, prominent citizens have also become important stamp collectors. Glenn Ford, a motion picture star, has collected valuable and rare stamps for many years. Ernest Borgnine, another movie star, is so great a stamp collector that he takes part in the U.S. stamp advisory committee, the group that selects the postage stamp designs. The Cardinal Spellman Philatelic Museum in Weston, Massachusetts received the late President Dwight D. Eisenhower's stamp collection after his death.

Prominent Canadians living from coast to coast have collected postage for 100 years or more. Professors, barristers, medical doctors and business people have all made names for themselves among philatelists. The Right Honorable Roland Michener, former Governor-General of Canada, is probably the best-known stamp collector in Canada.

The late J. Grant Glassco was one of the ten greatest philatelists in Canada. His name became a household word in the 1960s when he influenced all stamp collectors. Among scores of his recommendations he urged the Canada Post Office to stop the use of official stamps, airmails, and special delivery stamps. Mr. Glassco specialized in the history of the British postal services in America prior to the American Revolution.

If you have the Stamp Bug you are in good company. Good luck, good health and good collecting.

Douglas and Mary Patrick
August 15, 1978

This Canadian stamp from 1898
highlights the extent of the British
Empire at that time.
Stamps contain much historical
and geographical information.

1

FUN WITH STAMPS

Stamp collecting can provide pleasure and entertainment, as well as a broad education for anyone who has the desire to begin and the will to continue with the hobby.

John Robertson was one young man who found that what he learned from stamp collecting came in useful. He had applied for a job with a Canadian import-export company that did business in the West Indies. Among the eleven applicants, he was the only person who knew about the different countries and colonies in the Caribbean region of the world. In his stamp collection he saw stamps from Jamaica, Bahamas, St. Vincent, Barbados and other places. He realized they were British colonies at that time, about 1950, because the stamps were issued in British monetary denominations. The Dominican Republic and Haiti on the island of Hispaniola, he knew, were both independent countries where his prospective employer bought and

sold merchandise. Guadeloupe and Grande-Terre were French departments in the West Indies that used centimes and francs as their currency, and Curaçao, formerly a colony of the Netherlands north of Venezuela, had the Dutch currency of cents and gulden. John Robertson got the job because he was a stamp collector, a real Stamp Bug who learned geography and knew about the West Indian currencies from his postage stamps.

More people collect stamps than anything else in the world. Some people gather stamps in envelopes and boxes, but they are not real stamp collectors — they are nothing more than hoarders who fail to get the real pleasure that comes with stamp collecting. Any stamp collector, through his search for knowledge, can imagine himself in distant parts of the world, finding different people, strange customs and hundreds of well-known places. Some stamps also feature unusual products like the white pepper plants of Sarawak, oranges from Pitcairn Islands, orchids of the Philippines or the coconut palms of the Mozambique Company.

The Stamp Bug can really be an armchair traveller; he can go to any part of the world by turning a few pages in his album. Non-collectors never know such joy. Probably the greatest advantage in collecting stamps comes from the freedom each person enjoys. No one lays down set rules and insists that they be followed without variation. Each collector is his own director of his own collection, and does as he wishes. Stamp collecting is a field for adventure. And now is the time to procure the necessary materials to proceed.

These stamps represent various countries from the West Indies. One can learn about unfamiliar places from the pictures on stamps.

2

ESSENTIALS FOR A STAMP COLLECTION

Early in September, 1975, grandfather Wilmot bought his granddaughter an elaborate variety of stamp collecting materials, but some of them were for advanced collectors who had been in the hobby more than twenty-five years. Molly, a twelve-year-old, had decided to collect stamps and join the stamp club in her school.

Grandpa's gift included a $25 album, a black lamp worth $40, an electric watermark detector along with stamp tongs, hinges, and an electric magnifying glass. Molly didn't need most of these items.

Four things are really necessary and Molly Wilmot had the most important one — that is *desire*. It is the greatest asset any Stamp Bug can have. The other three are postage stamps, an album, and hinges to mount the stamps. Too many accessories can confuse a beginner and may spell the end to what could be a great adventure.

Other important accessories are tongs, a magnifier and, later when you are an experienced collector, a perforation gauge and a watermark detector. In a later chapter we describe how to make a stamp remover box that can be used safely to remove stamps of a fragile nature from paper and other materials. A book about collecting will become essential before many months. *Stamp Collecting,* by Stanley Phillips, published by Stanley Gibbons in London, England, is highly recommended. Borrow books about stamps from public libraries or from school libraries, but you must read, read, read, and absorb information to become a good stamp collector.

Albums

Forty years ago beginners were advised to buy albums with illustrated pages, but ideas and times have changed.

These album pages arranged by the stamp collector reflect his or her interest in a particular area. The two pages here show stamps of saints and portraits of important people.

Illustrated pages offer so many obstacles to the beginner that he is rarely able to make a presentable showing of the stamps he has. Poor illustrations on the pages often show more prominently than do the stamps themselves. It only confuses and discourages the beginners. If a Stamp Bug owns an album with pictures of stamps printed on the pages, he may use it and have fun filling in as many pages as possible with the stamps in his collection. When the time comes to mount a special showing of stamps for an exhibition or school work, he can remove the desired stamps from his album and remount them on the paper of his choice.

Stamp dealers have a variety of loose pages for stamp albums, ones that fit either three-ring binders or spring-back binders. The choice of the first album is not too important. A three-ring binder with blank pages or a small album sold by stamp

Three kinds of stamp albums

Printed album pages

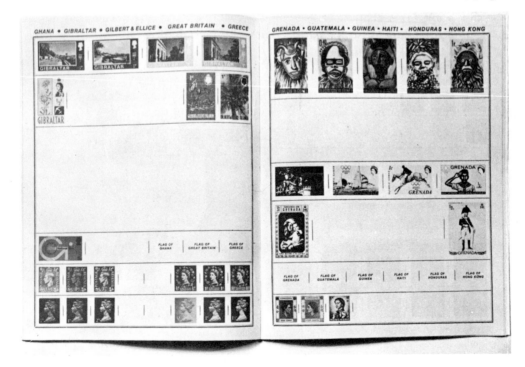

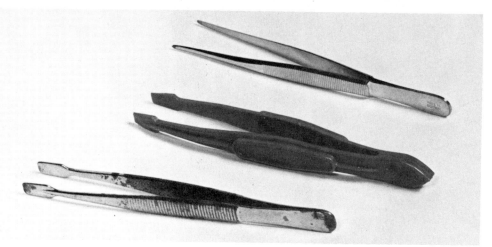

Here are various kinds of stamp tongs. Blunt ends are good to use because they are less likely to damage stamps. Pointed tipped tongs can be squeezed easily but you must be careful not to put the ends through the stamp.

dealers will serve as a first album. Beginners should avoid the huge 10-pound picture albums. As each collector advances he will change albums to suit his needs. One collector may have three or four different types of albums, some printed and specialized, others the blank loose-leaf kind. Good advice is to just start because everyone learns by doing.

Tongs

Stamp Bugs never handle dry stamps in their fingers for fear of damaging the stamps. Instead they use a special kind of tweezers called *stamp tongs*. The blunt ends of the tongs enable a collector to pick up and move stamps without damage. The best tongs are those that close easily and are not difficult to squeeze. Stiff tongs used for a few hours may cause tired fingers or wrists. Never use tongs to handle wet stamps, because they are fragile and easily punctured. Collectors should handle wet stamps with their fingers.

Stamp Hinges

Stamp hinges are most important to collectors. Stamp Bugs should not paste or glue stamps in any album. They should not use cellulose tape. Many valuable stamps have been ruined by uninformed people who stuck stamps down on a page with paste or tape.

Hinges should always be used in affixing stamps to album pages.

Sorting stamps
is the first step
in organizing
your collection.

Test a layout before affixing the
stamp to the page in case it might
look better elsewhere.

The safe way to mount stamps in an album is with hinges — little pieces of paper gummed on one side. Hinges are specially made with a gum that has several unusual qualities. The pure, nearly tasteless gum is applied to glassine paper hinges in a thin film. Thus the special gum carefully applied permits a collector to peel hinges from stamps and album pages without damaging page or stamp. Many collectors find the prefolded hinges useful time savers. Stamp dealers sell them.

If these directions are followed, a beginner will soon learn to mount stamps well and quickly.

1.   With tongs or fingers fold back and

Fold back the hinge.

Lick the bottom part of the hinge.

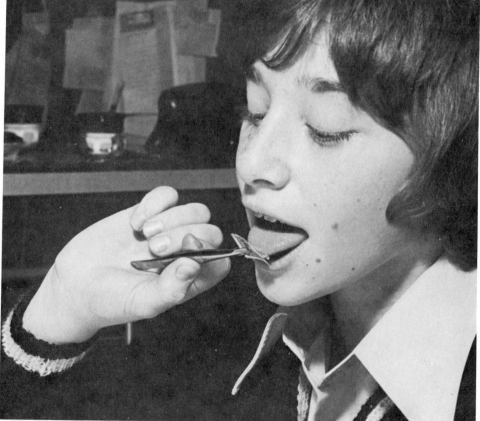

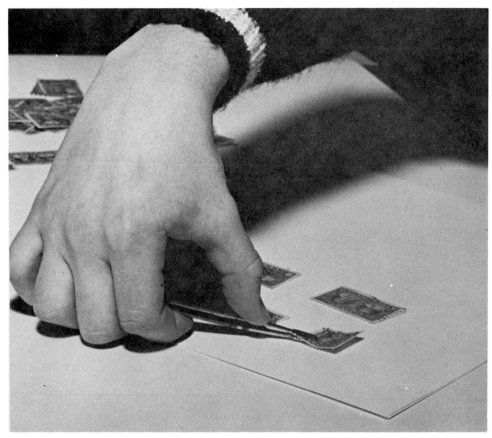

Place the stamp in position on the album page.

crease one-third of the hinge, the gum side or shiny side out. Prefolded hinges have the gum outside ready to use.

2. Moisten (not wet) the upper part of the one-third of the hinge. Apply this part of the hinge with the creased edge about one-eighth of an inch from the top perforations on the top back of the stamp.

3. Two-thirds of the hinge now stands at an angle from the stamp. Moisten (not wet) the bottom third of the hinge and place it carefully in the desired position on the page.

Never remove a hinge until it is dry (about one half-hour).
Never use cellulose tape as hinges.
Never stick down or paste stamps to pages. Always use hinges.

Here are pages from various types of stamp albums, from the hand-lettered to the printed.

Title Pages

A good stamp collection tells a story with postage stamps used as illustrations. Since every story, either long or short, should have a title page, stamp collections are no exception. The two examples shown here come from gold and silver-medal collections that had been shown in international stamp exhibitions.

Postmarks and Cancellations of India, **a collection arranged on nearly 700 pages, is divided into five distinctive sections: pre-stamp postal markings — from the reigns of Queen Victoria to King George VI. Indian postage stamps are so cheap this is an easy collection to form.**

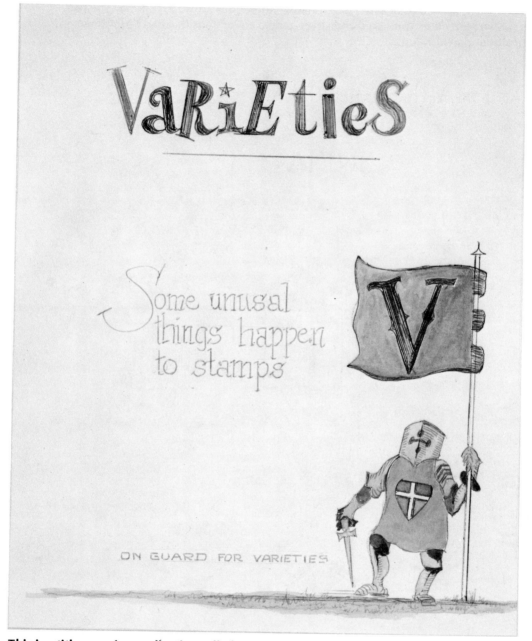

This is a title page for a collection called *Varieties*. **Varieties are everywhere. A variety collection is so easy to form that even a Stamp Bug of a few years can start a variety collection. But all collectors should beware of the ill-informed stamp dealers who try to sell common varieties as errors.**

3

HOW TO GET STAMPS

Friends can often supply collectors with interesting stamps and, of course, many companies get mail from all parts of the world. If you know someone who works in such a company, he may be willing to save stamps for you. You may also find stamps and old letters stashed away in old trunks and cupboards. Harry Rosenfeld bought a house in Toronto and found old mail in the attic — thousands of letters filed between the two-by-four-inch rafters. In his quiet way, he sold the old letters in different cities and by stamp auction and received more than he paid for the house. A knowledge of postage stamps and old letters has often led to huge profits.

People in cities and large towns may go to stamp shops or to stamp departments in department stores. The easiest way for people in small towns and rural areas to start a stamp collection is to buy a package of 500 or 1000 different stamps from any stamp dealer. Dealer names can be found in popular magazines, newspaper advertisements or in the yellow pages of the telephone book. Post office workers may provide the names of stamp collectors or dealers who patronize them. Junior Stamp Bugs should seek help from an adult.

Packages of assorted stamps fall into two classes: mixtures or all-different. Mixtures always contain duplicate stamps usually on pieces of their original paper complete with postal markings or cancellations. Mixtures often provide an inexpensive means of studying cancels, perforations, papers, and watermarks. In the past, mixtures have sometimes contained scarce stamps, but a collector should not rely on mixtures as a source of rarities.

The terms, *all-different* and *mixed* have been used for more than a hundred years. The first issue of the philatelic paper, *The Stamp Collectors Magazine* of February 1,

1863, contained two pages of classified advertisements for all-different packages of stamps. When the eleventh edition appeared in December, C. K. Jones advertised 5000 common stamps to the highest bidder.

As the years passed and people throughout the world graduated from the elementary style of collecting only one stamp of a kind, the popularity of mixtures increased. Stamp Bugs will soon discover that their duplicate stamps can be used for exchange. Quantities of one postage stamp may be valuable even though the price of a single stamp of the same type is small. Years ago a young collector, Albert Yeager, was given hundreds of five-cent Beaver-design stamps of Canada. He kept about fifteen for his collection and left the rest. He had no idea that local stamp dealers would have exchanged stamps for those he left behind. The moral is: Take all the stamps that people offer. You can exchange or sell them and buy others for your collection.

Duplicate stamps can have an added value. Collectors soon discover that their excess varieties can become a medium for making new friendships. Collectors enjoy exchanging stamps and even form clubs to help each other, to trade and learn more about collecting. Pleasure, entertainment, and new friends await beginners who will be welcomed at meetings of stamp clubs in his community. (See: How to Organize a Stamp Club.)

People who operate contests and coupon-redeeming companies get millions of stamps that come on replies to the contests and guessing games. Any person who knows an employee in such a company may bid on the used stamps and sell them to make money to buy stamps, books, and supplies for a better stamp collection. When Molly Deagon worked for a newspaper that ran a contest, she arranged for the people on the mailing desk to keep all the envelopes that came in. Molly obtained several hundred thousand letters this way, soaked off the stamps, bundled the good ones in packages of 100 each and sold them to a dealer for a total of $110. She spent the money buying tiles for her basement recreation-stamp room.

A Bag of Stamps

George Leydman worked more than six months delivering parcels for the local hardware dealer who collected stamps in a small central Ontario town. He worked without pay in order to get one bag of stamps. But this was no ordinary bag — it was a hundred pound sugar bag packed full of stamps that weighed more than thirty pounds. He tried to put the bag over the handlebars of his bicycle and ride at the same time, but he could not steer the bicycle with such a heavy weight, so he walked home with the bag slung between the handlebars. It was quite a struggle. He began to wonder what his mother would say when she saw such a tremendous number of stamps. He decided to go in the side door and up the back steps where no one in the family could see him.

When he got upstairs he dumped the contents of the bag into the bath tub and began pouring water on them. What a mess that made! Finally his mother came upstairs to see what he was doing and, split between anger and amusement, she decided not to spank him. She called her husband and the boy's two sisters and the five of them hauled the stamps out of the bathtub — some still dry but most of them wet — and placed them on a newspaper on the bathroom floor.

Well you never saw such an array of stamps and such confusion! George decided to soak the stamps a few at a time. He soaked them and sorted them. He had been collecting stamps at that time for several years and knew that if stamps were in a book they would be easier to sell than loose stamps. He got a big, inexpensive scribbler and started mounting the stamps right through from A to Z.

The stamps stayed around the house for two or three years before he was finished with them. He found some good stamps, and it was obvious that the people who had them originally had no idea what they were giving away. These stamps had been gathered for charity and the hardware dealer had bought them and then given them to young George. In the middle of the bag somewhere George found some really good stamps — $5 Columbia Exposition stamp of the United States, $1 and $4 Canadian Jubilees, as well as lower values, and he also found some British £1 King Edward VII stamps.

In 1916-20 none of these stamps were really expensive in the way they are today. The $5 Columbian was listed at $1.75 used, and the $4 one at $6 used. The British stamp, the £1 horizontal green stamp, was listed at $6 used, considerably lower than these stamps are worth today.

Finally, after working for more than two years, George managed to salvage the entire bag of stamps. On looking back he was amused by the fact that he took the bag of stamps home and dumped them in the bathtub all at one time. He did this because he lacked experience. The contents of the bag probably numbered 70 000 stamps on paper and hundreds of them — as there are in all big mixtures — were damaged and useless. He threw these away.

Other Places to Get Stamps

Time will come when the Stamp Bug wants stamps that are not available through normal exchange or from other sources. Apart from the all-different stamp packages mentioned earlier, dealers also sell stamps by *want lists* to customers who establish credit. This

This is a 5¢ Beaver stamp issued in 1859. Notice the circular date stamp, "London, Canada West, March 6, 1867," the year of Confederation.

These are approvals from the Empire Stamp Corp. and the Garcelon Stamp Co.

means that a dealer will send the stamps you order and you send him the money. Every year hundreds of thousands of dollars pass through the mail in payment of postage stamps and collectors' supplies that collectors have requested. Such large purchases by mail are a tribute to the integrity of stamp collectors.

Some of the big stamp dealers in the United States and Great Britain still send approvals to collectors who request them.

These dealers often hire handicapped people to mount the stamps thus providing employment and good wages to these people.

A great many collectors seem reluctant to talk about their stamps to people when they have the opportunity, but advertising the fact that you collect stamps is often worth the effort. Jewellery with stamp designs, for instance, will let others know that you collect stamps.

Two outstanding examples prove the success of this form of advertisement — the late Charles Moore wore a plastic pin of the CBC stamp club on the front of his ski cap one day and at the crest of a hill another man saw the button and asked Mr. Moore about his collecting activities. The outcome proved most profitable when Mr. Moore received a gift of several thousand British stamps that were his collecting specialty.

Some years ago Robert Blatchford sat down to dinner aboard a train in western Canada. He was wearing a Society of Philatelic Americans pin that his tablemate recognized and they began talking about postage stamps. As a result Mr. Blatchford was able to buy a valuable collection. In fact the money involved in the purchase of a twenty-five-volume collection of British Commonwealth stamps ran into six figures.

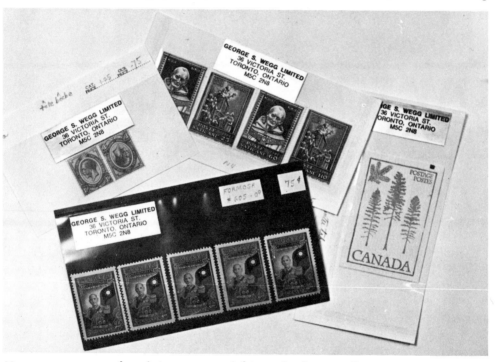

Here are some samples of stamps you might receive by want lists.

4

HOW TO REMOVE STAMPS

Every Stamp Bug must know how to remove stamps from paper and how to avoid damaging the stamps. When stamps are torn from envelopes or wrapping paper, half an inch or more must be left to protect the edges of the stamps. Another important warning: stamps should never be pulled off paper. A non-collector might direct a beginner to steam the stamps from paper. If 10 000 stamps had to be removed this way it would take years and nobody should spend a long time on such a trivial job when only hours are needed to soak the stamps off.

A container, some cold water, several clean newspapers, and plenty of space (a table is good) are required for the process of removing stamps from paper. A container such as a washbasin or saucepan should be large enough to permit the stamps and

paper to float in it. One hundred stamps cannot easily be soaked off paper if they are placed in an ordinary drinking glass.

Experienced collectors place the stamps in the container, run cold water over them until they float around, and let them soak from ten to thirty minutes. In this way the stamps will not be crushed or torn. Wet stamps are easily damaged. Work carefully.

When the stamps have soaked, some may have separated from the papers. The pieces of paper should be carefully examined on both sides before they are discarded, since the face of a stamp will attach itself to another piece of paper in the water. Often the water used in floating off the stamps becomes dirty, and you'll need fresh water. At least one change of water will be needed when hundreds of stamps are being soaked.

Soaking stamps in water is a good way to remove them from paper.

Stamps should not be lost when the water is poured off. When all the stamps have separated from the papers, the papers should be discarded, leaving the stamps floating in the water. Then the water may be changed again or the stamps may be carefully removed into another container filled with clean water.

The next step is to remove the stamps from the water and place them on an open, clean, dry newspaper page. When all of the stamps have been laid carefully to avoid any creases, the other half of the page should be laid over the wet stamps. These papers should be put away flat either with or without a weight on them. One collector

dries his stamps between newspapers under the bedroom rug.

Some collectors have lost good stamps by drying them in books and forgetting where they were placed. Herbert Davis was examining books in a secondhand store and found a Canadian 3-penny stamp on laid paper (1851) in a tattered novel. It was worth about $35 at the time.

Certain stamps, notably those of the former Dutch Indies, are printed with ink that runs in water, and special care is therefore needed to remove them from paper, using the stamp remover box described later on. Some stamps from the British Commonwealth have been printed on chalk-surfaced paper (chalky paper); these also need expert handling with the stamp remover box. Postage stamp catalogues identify stamps that are on chalky paper.

Care should be taken to avoid soaking off stamps stuck on green, purple, or other dark-coloured wrapping papers. The dye frequently comes out of the wrapping paper and tints the stamps. No collector wants artificially tinted stamps in his collection. Separating the stamps on coloured paper from the others is a way to avoid damage. Green wrapping paper is the most frequent offender. All stamps on coloured papers should be removed separately or in a stamp remover box (described in the next chapter). If the colours run and tint the stamps, then the stamps are useless and are classified as damaged. A stamp remover box separates all stamps without causing the colours to run.

Some stamps have been mounted so many times that several parts of hinges remain stuck to them. Such hinges are removed from used stamps in the same way as other paper. An experienced collector should be consulted about lifting stuck-

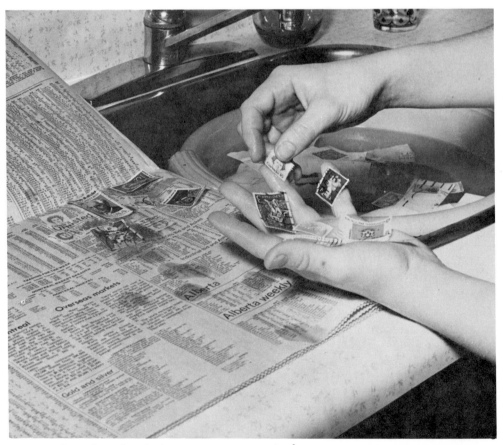

You can then place the stamps on a newspaper to dry.

These stamps are being left between the newspaper pages to be pressed.

down stamps from album pages or removing many hinges from unused stamps. Warning — such a job is most difficult and should be undertaken only when the owner realizes that even with the most intelligent care his stamp may be ruined.

Fugitive Cancellations

Stamp Bugs are sure to learn that collecting has its own language. The word fugitive is used for cancellations that run when stamps are submerged in water and thus tint or colour the faces of the stamps themselves and others nearby. Collectors should avoid stamps that have been damaged by incorrect methods of removing them from paper, and should take special care in removing stamps with cancels that may run.

Anne Patterson wrote a tearful letter after she had lost some stamps by soaking them in water. She didn't know that the pretty, purple postmarks would run and ruin her stamps.

The coloured cancellations on stamps from Canada, South America, and especially Venezuela are those to watch. The beginner

Here is a red fugitive cancel which is blurred at the left side of the stamp.

ought not to be afraid to approach the job of removing the stamps so cancelled, but the task does require a little patience. Not all coloured cancellations run. Several hundred Canadian stamps with coloured cancellations were soaked off paper. Only four cancellations ran, and the colours were not strong enough to destroy other stamps in the bath.

For a great many stamps, the following procedure can be used. Dry absorbent paper is placed on a flat surface; the stamps are then placed face (picture side) down on the dry paper. Wet white paper is placed over the lot and pressed with any heavy object. If these stamps are left overnight, on the following morning they can be lifted without blurring the fugitive cancellations.

Each collector should experiment in order to find the best method suited to his purpose. Rare and expensive stamps should be handled carefully and only after practice has been gained by experiments with inexpensive stamps.

An experienced collector sometimes moistens his thumb on his tongue and repeatedly presses his moist thumb against the paper bearing the stamp. He can quickly lift an ordinary stamp. But, after all, he has had years of experience.

5

THE STAMP
REMOVER
BOX

Sooner or later every stamp collector will be faced with the problem of wanting to remove stamps without submerging them in water. There are many reasons for this and the answer to the problem is a stamp remover box. You can, of course, buy one of these boxes, but if you prefer to save five or six dollars, you can make your own. It's easy. You can get the materials from odds and ends around the house.

The three main items that you need are a box with a tight-fitting lid, a rack, grill, or grid that fits in the box, and a sponge or cloth. It is important that these materials be made of non-rusting material. In addition, it's helpful if they are transparent, so that you can see what is occurring inside the box. This suggests see-through plastic as the best material, but good boxes can be made from opaque plastics like the butter boxes and margarine containers available in any supermarket.

The box should be large enough to hold one small business-size envelope, about four by six inches. Keeping this in mind, your box could measure about five by seven by two inches, but it could be larger or smaller, depending on how you expect to use it. It need not even be square, oblong, or rectangular; it could be circular. But, whatever the shape, it must have a close-fitting lid.

The rack can be made most easily from one of those common fruit baskets approximately four or five inches square and three inches deep. They often hold strawberries, raspberries, or vegetables. They are light, can be easily cut to the right

**Stamp remover box and
sponge**

**Stamp remover box
and stamps**

size, and do not rust. The purpose of the rack is to keep the stamp and its cover out of contact with anything that is wet.

Either a sponge or wet cloth can be used as a source of moisture. This moisture becomes the effective agent in loosening the gum that sticks the stamp to its cover.

To use the box, place the wet sponge or

cloth in the bottom, then insert the rack. Lay the stamp on the rack, place the lid on the box, and wait for the moisture to work on the stamp's adhesive. The process takes anywhere from a half-hour to a day, usually from six to twenty-four hours. It can be speeded up if you use hot water on the sponge or cloth, and if there is a tight seal on the lid of the box so that no moisture escapes.

When the softening process is finished, you must, of course, be extremely careful in removing the stamp from the paper. It is best done by hand; tongs might puncture the stamp. With a little practice you'll become skilful in removing the stamp from its envelope. You may find that the gum holding the envelope together may also loosen somewhat, but you can easily re-stick the envelope as soon as it is removed from the box.

When the stamp is off you can examine it for watermarks, perforations, faults, or type of paper. Then you can, if you wish, return the stamp to its original position on the envelope. With practice you'll be able to replace it so carefully and skilfully that you can even match the cancellation marks on the stamp and on the adjoining paper of the envelope.

Try a number of experiments, using your box or various types of boxes, until you become proficient at removing stamps without water. You'll find that the use of this stamp strip-easy box is a breeze.

Using the Remover Box

Stamps coming from the box can be dried flat between pieces of plastic food wrapping. Use a light weight on top to prevent the stamp from curling. It is necessary to use the plastic on both the gummed and face sides, as the weight will squish some gum out between the perforations.

The box works well for removing stubborn hinges from mint stamps. You may have to return the stamp to the box several times if it dries before you have been able to remove the entire hinge. The stamp is left with the gum somewhat disturbed but it's better than risking a thinned spot by peeling off a dry hinge. Mr. Wegg makes this suggestion: "Certain stamps, such as the Edward VII Issue of Canada, are quite porous and two minutes too long in the box allows the gum to soak into the stamps and stain them permanently."

If a lot of gum is left on a used stamp, you can remove most of it by gently wiping the back with a damp sponge. Lay it face down on the plastic while you wipe it. Then dry it between the plastic wrapping sheets, as even wiping it will not remove the gum.

Be careful not to leave the stamp in the box too long if it is on brown wrapping paper or if there is an ink mark under the stamp. Some yellow dye from the paper may stain the stamp and the ink mark may also stain it.

6

SORTING STAMPS

Sooner or later every stamp collector must sort stamps and, as with other activities in the hobby, there are no set rules on exactly how to do it. Every collector finds his own preferred method of sorting postage stamps. Beginners, however, must have a starting point.

Here's one idea. Spread the stamps face up on a dry, clean surface and make separate piles for each country. Make another pile for unidentified stamps, and don't let this discourage you because even advanced philatelists have difficulty telling the origin of some postage stamps. There are so many languages and so many different alphabets that the ability to say that this stamp comes from Israel or from the Indian Native States or from some other place comes only with experience. Some postage stamps are difficult to identify because the most prominent word is not

always the country's name. Other stamps have unfamiliar foreign names printed in native languages. Refer to the glossary at the back of this book for help in distinguishing the origin of stamps.

Mr. Wegg says: "Storing stamps in envelopes can be a real bottleneck. I would suggest encouraging the collector to use 8½ x 11 stock sheets which fit a three-ring binder wherever possible, only resorting to the use of envelopes for storing any surpluses involving a hundred or more of any one stamp."

The unidentified pile must be handled separately. Place the stamps that appear to have the same lettering or alphabet in individual piles. Some English word on each stamp may help to classify a certain stamp. For example, stamps with the Oriental words and the English word "cents" may have come from China; those with "sen" or

The 8½ x 11 stock sheet has pockets which are used for storing stamps before the stamps are mounted in an album.

"yen" are from Japan. United Arab Republic (U.A.R.) stamps inscribed in Arabic also include English or French spellings of the country names.

After you have sorted all your stamps and set your problem stamps aside, consult the glossary again because it can be an extremely handy tool for you even after you have become an advanced collector. Then, when you know the country of origin, you can consult a postage stamp catalogue or a stamp dictionary and see illustrations of postage stamps. Your stamp may be illustrated in one of these books. If you don't own a catalogue you can borrow one from a library. In Canada, these have proved to be the most popular stamp books in libraries.

Stamp Bugs should consult the glossary when they encounter names of countries they don't recognize. This Czechoslovakian stamp commemorates the Olympic Games in Mexico in 1970, and is cancelled to order.

This is a souvenir sheet of Japanese stamps issued in 1962. In modern Japanese stamps, the first character is shaped like the figure 8.

Korean stamps can be distinguished by the circle containing two "apostrophes." They represent the yin and yang, symbols of the two opposing principles of existence, e.g. night and day, life and death, male and female.

7

MOUNT A PRIZE-WINNING COLLECTION

An arrangement of postage stamps on an album page may be a success or a dismal failure depending on the collector's knowledge and experience, and the care that he uses. On this subject, Max Werner, an art instructor, offers suggestions and comments: "One of the saddest things I know is any collection of postage stamps written up in a bad fashion on poor album pages. As I see it, several basic rules concern the write-up of stamp album pages, and I'll attempt to list these in chronological order.

"A simple page is best for mounting stamps; these range in price from $5 per hundred to 25c or more per page. The cheaper the pages are, frequently the more meaningless ornamentation they have. With a suitable quadrille sheet the first step is to lay out the stamps on the page without applying hinges — dry, in other words. This is the time to decide what text goes on the pages, whether it be a story or merely a date of issue, or something in between these extremes.

"In placing the stamps on the page, there are a few rules worth following. A single stamp, for instance, should not be placed exactly in the centre; it's better slightly above the centre, allowing for text to be lettered near it. Never mount stamps on an

ABCDEFGHIJKLM
NOPQRSTUVWXYZ

abcdefghijklmnopqrstuvwxyz
123456789

ABCDEFGHIJKLM
NOPQRSTUVWXYZ

abcdefghijklmnopqrstuvwxyz

1234567890

A B C D E F G H I J K L M N O P Q R S T U V W X Y Z

a b c d e f g h i j k l m n o p q r s t u v w x y z 1 2 3 4 5 6 7 8 9 0

Above you can see various typefaces that can be used when mounting your collection. You can use either hand-lettering or Letraset, which are printed letters that can be transferred onto the page.

angle, for they were not intended to be viewed in that way.

"There is much to be said for the symmetrical mounting of stamps, but it is not absolutely necessary. A non-symmetrical arrangement can be just as pleasing if it is well balanced. Some collectors prefer to draw thin lines around the stamps or covers on album pages. This can be done with a ruling pen or a sharp pencil of hardness H."

Lettering and Typing

After the layout and copy have been decided, the time for lettering is at hand. Most people who can write can also letter, especially with the help of the *Speedball Text Book,* a beginner's guide by Ross F. George. The lettering may be done with India or Chinese ink or even with a well-sharpened pencil to ensure uniform line thickness. Sepia waterproof drawing ink is strongly recommended; blue, red, or green inks may clash with the colours of postage stamps and should, under most circumstances, be avoided. Typewritten text looks better if it is typed right on the album pages instead of on the pasted-down strips so often seen in stamp shows. Collectors may wish to type the text on another piece of paper first to determine the size of space required as well as the location of the words on the album pages.

Finally, a few words of caution: avoid Olde English and similar ornate alphabets; choose a block lettering like that on architects' or draftsmen's drawings. Do not make the letters too large; 3/32 of an inch is recommended. Above all, do the lettering before the stamps are finally mounted, as an ink spot on a rare stamp means a tragic end to what should be a pleasant adventure. If arrows are required, be careful to choose colours that harmonize with the postage stamp colour. You'll always be safe in using black or grey arrows. Better still, with a fine pen, draw little arrows, one horizontal and another vertical, pointing to the exact spot of interest. Finally, I suggest that the most important object on any stamp page is the stamp itself.

WRITE-UP

Junior Stamp Bugs may take a few lessons from advanced stamp collectors who use a typewriter for their text that describes their stamps or covers. They call these words their write-up. The typewriting is so much better than poor hand writing or shaky hand lettering of an inexperienced person. The write-up may be typewritten directly on stamp album pages or on tiny pieces of thin cardboard or heavy papers. Experienced collectors arrange the stamps covers and related materials first before they prepare their descriptive text. They place the write-up below the materials on their pages. The text should be accurate and short for easy understanding at stamp exhibitions.

8

POST OFFICE LANGUAGE*

The postal service has developed a language of its own. Through the centuries English has absorbed words associated with the postal system, such as the word post itself. It comes from the Latin *posita*, from the infinitive *ponere*, to place. Posts were stations or houses located at fixed distances along the roads used by the couriers or coaches transporting mail. These posts or post houses may have been thatch-roofed cottages, inns, or larger buildings with barns to house horses and coaches.

The title postmaster came from King Henry VIII. He created the office of "Master of the Postes" early in the sixteenth century, and Brian Tuke held the position in the British realm as early as 1516. He had charge of the post horses, the post men (or boys, depending on their age), and he was also Keeper of the Post House.

The post office was originally a room in the post house or inn of the postmaster. Sometimes the post office merely occupied a corner in a room of a dirty little hut used to shelter a family and even a few of their animals. Under any circumstances the post office served as a place set aside to receive and hand out letters which had been delivered along one or more stages. These stages were the distance from one post house to another.

Thus the word postage came into use. Postage meant the fee paid to postmasters to have their post riders carry letters over one or more post stages. In a similar way the stage coach originated as a wagon used to carry freight, passengers, and letters over the stages or roads used by the masters of the posts.

The word mail comes from an Old French word, *malle*, which was a kind of saddle bag used by the post riders to carry letters. The

*From an interview with James Goodwin, postal historian.

bags were made of leather and lined with cotton or baize. Many years later the word malle became anglicized, first to male, then to maile, and finally, mail. The Royal Mail, therefore, originally meant the Royal Letter Bag, but now the term refers to the entire postal system throughout the British Commonwealth.

To post or mail a letter originally meant to hand the letter to the postmaster at the post house and leave it in his care for delivery. For the fee paid to him — postage — he was obliged to place the letters in the official postage saddle bag for its conveyance to the next destination by the authorized post rider.

The word sincerely had an earlier origin than other postal terms. In the days of the Roman Empire, an officer wishing to send reports or correspondence to another would often leave his message unsealed — that is, without the sealing wax used in those days to seal letters. The Latin word for without is *sine*, and *cera* means wax. Hence if a

messenger carried a letter without wax to seal it, he was a trusted servant. Three other explanations of the origin of sincerely exist, but this one seems logical for a story of postal history.

The Romans developed various writing customs described by words now commonly used in English. Julius Caesar began the custom of folding the letter sheets and writing on each folded page separately. The consuls and generals before him had written letters across an entire sheet on one side, but the people followed the example set by Caesar and folded their messages. The folded sheet was called a diploma, meaning double fold.

Because writing material was relatively rare, the Romans most frequently used small tablets. These tablets were often elaborately framed, with the inner part made of wood or ivory covered with white or coloured wax. The writer inscribed his words in the wax surface by means of a small metal rod called a style. The end of the style used for writing was pointed; the opposite end resembled a chisel and was used to flatten the wax to erase words.

The Roman gentleman always carried his style and writing tablet with him. Because he could not wear a sword or dagger within the city, the style became a handy weapon for protection during a heated argument. The gentleman's descendants converted the weapon into the small sharp knife, called a stiletto.

The Egyptians provided their share of words for postal items. The best of all the primitive forerunners of paper was formed from a plant somewhat like North American bullrushes that grew in wet places. In Egypt the plant was called *papyrus*, and from it comes the English word paper. The

Here is a first day cancel on a stamp showing a stagecoach used for delivering mail.

Egyptians unfolded the membranes of the plant, laid them out straight, and then crossed the first rows with more fibres. They moistened and then pressed the entire mass. After the substance dried, a workman burnished the better side by using a boar tusk. And from this action comes the term *Charta dentata* of Cicero — loosely translated as paper made with the aid of a tooth.

The ancient people kept the finished papyrus, with the inscriptions on them, in rolls like maps on rollers today. These scrolls were unrolled by the person reading them.

The English word volume comes from the Latin *volumen,* meaning scroll.

When the Egyptians discovered that a literary student in Pergamus in Asia Minor had a library comparable to those of the Ptolemies (Greek kings of Egypt about 323 to 30 BC), exports of papyrus were forbidden. The people of Asia Minor by necessity improving their tanning methods, manufactured *pergamena* from sheep and goat skins; hence our word parchment. The tanned skins of calves became known as *villum* and a trace of the similarity remains in the words vellum and veal.

These Norwegian stamps show the post horn which was used to announce the arrival of the stage coach before reaching the stage.

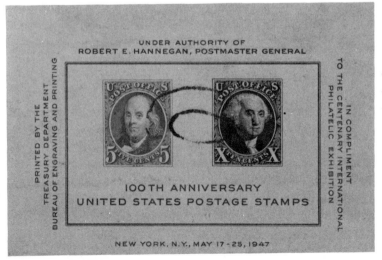

U.S. souvenir sheet to commemorate the 100th anniversary of U.S. postage stamps, 1947.

9

HOW TO ORGANIZE A STAMP CLUB

The requirements for a stamp club are simple: first is desire; second is a group of serious collectors, boys, girls, men, women, or mixed groups — boys and girls, school-aged children, or adult men and women. Any group considering the formation of a stamp club may be well advised to seek the help of an experienced stamp collector, if the group does not include one.

The following suggestions are intended to help, but may not necessarily be the final states in the establishment of a stamp club. First the group must agree on the meeting date, time, and place. Although it may not always be possible, a group should try to have its meeting in the same place, at the same time, and at regular intervals, whether they be bi-monthly, monthly, or even weekly. The meetings may be held in a home, a schoolroom, a church, or in some local hall; everything depends on the circumstances of the group.

Constitution

After a few informal meetings, when the members get to know one another, an election of officers is highly recommended. A suggested executive for a large group would be president, vice-president, secretary, treasurer, and a membership convener. An extremely small group could confine its executive to a president and a secretary-treasurer. Parliamentary procedure could be followed in conducting the meetings. Young people especially seem to thrive on a moderately and reasonably disciplined meeting.

Seaplane Flight
Australia – Japan
F. C. Chichester
1931.

VIA AIR MAIL

338

FOR THIS LETTER IS NO. 338 OF 872
LETTERS CARRIED FROM MANILA TO KATSUURA JAPAN
ON THE WORLD'S FIRST LONG-DISTANCE SEAPLANE
SOLO AND FIRST SOLO FLIGHT AUSTRALIA-JAPAN. THEY
WERE CARRIED TO JAPAN AND NO FURTHER OWING
TO THE TOTAL WRECK THERE OF MY PLANE AND
WERE THE ONLY LETTERS CARRIED INTERNATIONALLY
AFTER AUSTRALIA EXCEPT FOR THE 145 CARRIED
FROM AUSTRALIA AND THE 10 FROM MANILA TO
SHANGHAI CHINA.

Francis C. Chichester

W. BRUGGMANN, Esq.

c/o. F.C. Chichester
British Aviator

CANADA

July 27, 1931 cover from Manila to Japan with
Japanese arrival mark on reverse side.

Rare cover sent from Manila to Japan flown by the late Sir Francis Chichester who sailed around the world. This page is from a prize-winning collection. The first sentence, which is partially illegible, reads, ''This letter is no. 338 of 872 carried from Manila to Katsuura Japan on the world's first long distance seaplane solo and first solo flight Australia — Japan.''

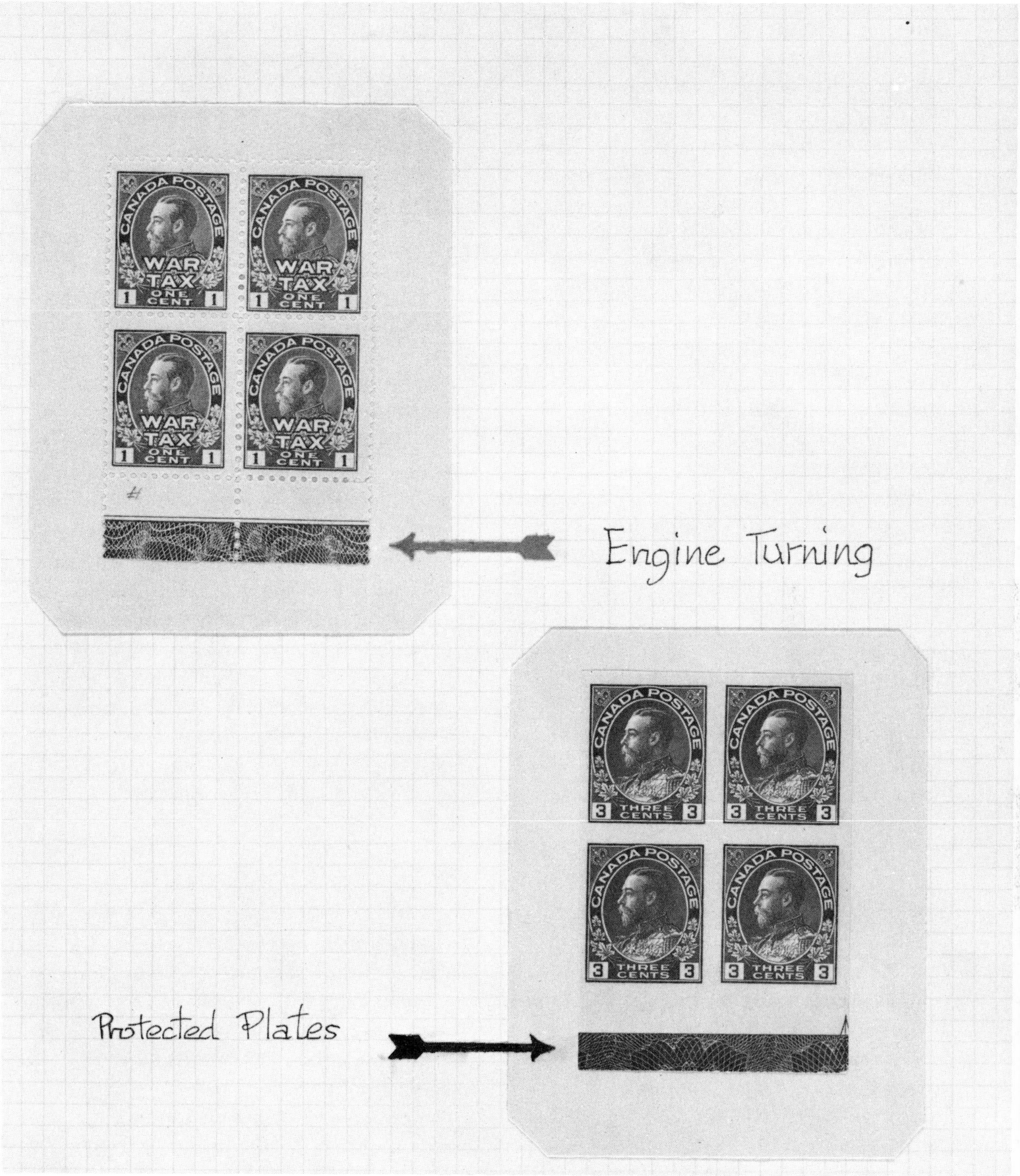

Engine Turning

Protected Plates

These two blocks show engine turning or geometric engraving, i.e. the machine engraving of intricate, symmetrical patterns on metal. The machine engraves the stamp to a uniform depth — a feat that no person can accomplish by hand.

Dues and Finances

Experience has proven that a membership fee is essential. The members themselves feel that they have a part or a stake in the club. When they have paid a membership fee, they should receive a membership card. While dues may be kept at a minimum, the operators of the club must consider their own expenses. The rent of the hall, or any other expenses that come along, must be paid. The exact amount of a fee should be determined at some group meeting. No set amount can be established here, as expenses vary so greatly from one place to another, as do the expenses of each individual group. One group may wish to meet in a hotel room, another group in a church hall or in a library, where the rental fee would be much less.

Creating a Centre of Interest

One of the essentials in establishing a stamp club is the creation of a centre of interest for the members. Even this centre of interest may vary from one group to another. A junior group will likely require postage stamp catalogues. A subscription to one of the popular stamp magazines is also a great help to a junior group. Most adult groups have members who subscribe to stamp journals or newspapers, and who also have their own catalogues. Those who do not have catalogues often borrow them from other members or from a library.

Inexpensive catalogues can be had in Canada. For example, the *Lyman's Canada Catalogue*, published annually, is a good one. The H. E. Harris Company in Boston, Mass., publishes a United States, United Nations, and British North America catalogue. George Wegg says: "I think the *Canada Specialized Catalogue* is an informative book more accurate in its pricing. Another book I recommend to collectors after they advance is *The Fundamentals of Philately* by L. N. and M. Williams."

Stanley Gibbons of London, England, produces unusual catalogues of Britain and the Channel Islands that are checklists. These books all sell for moderate prices and may be procured through the publishers themselves, through stamp dealers, or in some cases, at bookstores.

Collectors must learn the fundamentals of collecting and here books become essential. One outstanding example, and necessary in every philatelic library, is *How to Arrange and Write Up a Stamp Collection* by Stanley Phillips and C. P. Rang. Stanley Gibbons of London has published this for many years. *Stamp Collecting* by the late Stanley Phillips, also published by Stanley Gibbons, answers hundreds of questions that stamp collectors ask. Another highly recommended book is *Stamps — Their Lure and Lore* by Ken Conoley, published by Longmans Canada Ltd., in Toronto, Ontario, Canada.

Have fun at stamp club meetings. Some clubs hold auction sales about once a month. They should not be held too often, because frequency spoils the fun of the sales. A trading session may be provided at each meeting; some clubs hold them before the meeting starts. This again is up to the individual club and the status of its advancement.

Members of the club should always remember that money is not an objective in stamp collecting. It is at the most an asset. Any collector can have just as much pleasure with twenty-five cents' worth of stamps as he could with a hundred dollars'

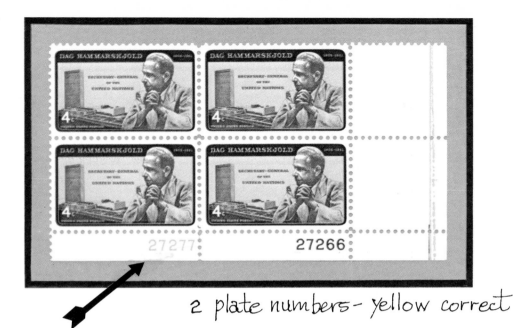

2 plate numbers – yellow correct

yellow inverted

Notice the colour error in the lower block of stamps (the yellow comes in the wrong place). This error was reprinted following its discovery, to reduce its value in the stamp market.

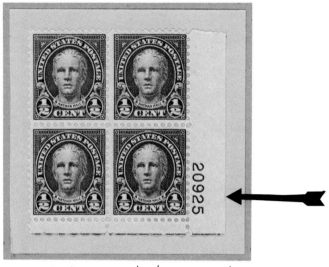

Rotary plate number

Flat plate number with F

These two blocks show the U.S. plate numbers, rotary on the side margin, and the flat plate on the top or bottom margin.

Three-color plate numbers. Bars are co-extensive lines to protect plate—

Centre-line arrow, co-extensive lines and eight registration marks in colors on the stamps.

The top block shows the three different plate numbers with their corresponding colours. The bottom show eight different colours including yellow, which is hardly visible. The "Blue Tit" was often thought to be an error because it is shown upside down. In fact, it is correct because that is the way it feeds.

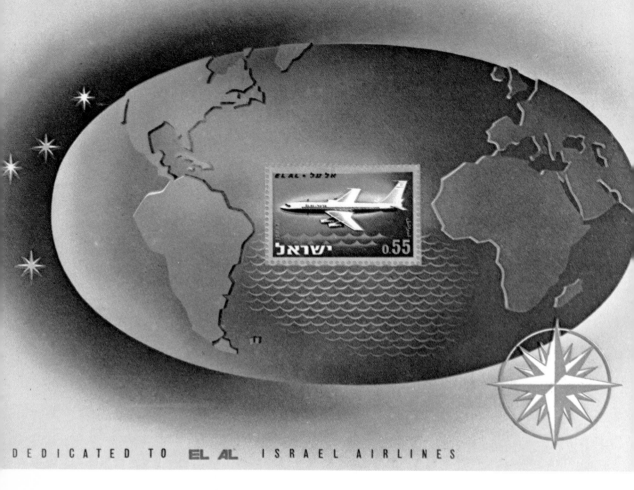

מוקדש ל אל על נתיבי אויר לישראל

DEDICATED TO EL AL ISRAEL AIRLINES

This Israeli souvenir sheet showing a Boeing 707 was issued to publicize the El Al airline on Nov. 7, 1962 in connection with the El Al philatelic exhibition in Tel Aviv.

This is a Japanese souvenir sheet, issued for the New Year on Jan. 20, 1966. It shows the "secret horse straw toy" of Japan. At the side of the block notice the delicate decorative work.

worth. In fact, a collector needs a great deal of skill to win a prize for a collection with a low-value display of postage stamps. The late Albert Bradley used to say that a collector is better off owning a hundred stamps and knowing something about each one of them, than he is if he owns 10 000 and knows nothing about any of them.

The directors of a stamp club should arrange for good speakers and good entertainment; sometimes games prove beneficial. Instructions, including the use of stamp hinges, may be helpful. An amazing number of adult collectors do not know how to hinge a stamp properly. Beginners should learn the useful art of soaking stamps, and which stamps not to soak.

A quiz program creates a great deal of fun if all the members participate. They should be urged to take part, so that nobody is a wallflower. About twenty questions with stamps or facts to provide the answers will entertain the members all night.

The success of any stamp club comes in direct proportion to the degree of participation of all its members. Members don't like to sit on the sidelines and look on. They far prefer to take part. Encourage shy members to participate. Programs designed to give every member a chance to take part are usually the most successful for a stamp club, whether it is an established group or one just beginning.

As time passes the club members may wish to hold a stamp exhibition.

10

SEEKING HELP

When some readers ask questions about stamps, collecting problems or postal history, they often apologize for not knowing the answers, especially if they think the questions are simple.

Sometimes the questions that sound easy are the most difficult to answer, for example, "How many stamps has Canada issued?" A brief discussion of that question would require about six pages, a complete one could fill more than fifty.

Collectors should never be reluctant to ask questions, apart from those involving values, because no person knows all the answers to questions about the 250 000 different stamps issued in the world since 1840, or about the postal history of the past four hundred years. Appraisals of the value of stamps must be made by professional philatelists, who charge a nominal fee for their work. Any attempt to get free valuations is futile.

Typical questions range anywhere from those regarding cleaning to queries about historical figures. For example, one collector asked about removing cellulose tape from postage stamps. Cellulose tape usually soaks off postage stamps if they are left in water for a half-hour or longer. Collectors should avoid rubbing the sticky material from the stamps, for it will soak off if the stamps are left in the water. This tape should never be used to mount stamps or covers.

Grease stains may be removed by carefully submerging the stamps in carbon tetrachloride (where it can be used legally), rubbing alcohol, or benzine. But remember that wet stamps are exceptionally fragile, and no issues printed by gravure should be submerged or cleaned with those three solvents, which dissolve some of the gravure printing inks.

The powdered detergents may dissolve certain grease stains from postage stamp paper. But use household cleansers with great care; one teaspoonful in two quarts of water should be a maximum solution. Stamps submerged in this solution for fifteen seconds will probably be free of grease spots. Time for experimenting is absolutely necessary, and anyone who attempts to clean his own stamps does so at his own risk.

One collector had difficulty finding information about Jean Talon, portrayed on Canadian postage stamps issued on June 13, 1962. History books provide the answers. During the years 1665-68, Jean Talon served as intendant of New France. Among his numerous achievements, he discovered a shortage of women in the colony and requested that 1000 carefully selected girls

come to Canada to become wives of the men in the colony. The illustration on the stamp depicts his gift to each married couple: a bull, cow, hog, sow, cock, and hen. He is also shown giving a couple of barrels of salt meat and eleven crowns.

The never-ending flow of questions about postage stamps helps to keep stamp collecting a fascinating pastime. For example: "Canada issued four-cent wartime design postage stamps imperforate top and bottom, but perforated twelve vertically. Are these errors in coil stamps?" No. This series of postage stamps resembling coil postage all came from various booklet panes of three stamps each. (Some collectors called them the chewing-gum booklets owing to their shape.) The two stamps at

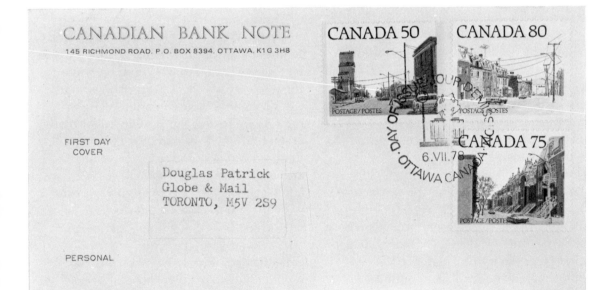

Here is a First Day Cover used as an advertisement for the Canadian Bank Note Company, Limited. Collectors can obtain their own First Day Covers by buying stamps from the Post Office on the first day of the stamp issue and mailing a letter to themselves. The cancellation will then show the date of the issue.

the left side of each pane resemble coils, while the third stamp is not perforated on the right side.

"Where does a blue-colour stamp come from with the name Republica Populara Romana?" These stamps are from Romania, despite the spelling. Most Romanian postage stamps are inscribed Romania or Romina.

"Is a first-day cover postmarked before the official date of issue rare or more valuable than one dated on the correct day?" No. Stamp collectors who specialize in individual subjects generally look on early dated covers as manufactured products, and on this basis they reject such covers. The covers are not classified as rare because fakers who alter philatelic items to enhance the values could make covers like these at any time, especially with help from a post office clerk. Collectors should never pay extra for such dubious products.

"Are the three 1958 postage stamps of Ghana which sold without authorization in 1957 rare stamps if they are cancelled with a dated postmark of 1957?" Once again the answer is no. The three stamps from two- to four-pence may be cancelled 1957 by fakers who would intentionally cancel the stamps to procure higher prices.

Like the pre-dated covers, these Ghana stamps and others that may be similar are frowned on by purists. No real student of philately would deliberately indulge in these made-to-order products. The stamp dealers refrain from such trivial material, but unfortunately the small, ill-informed collector who has become a vest-pocket

dealer may try to sell these items. Therefore collectors are advised to deal with established stamp dealers who have proper business locations and ethical standards to maintain.

Many questions may be answered in the popular stamp catalogues available in libraries. Exceptions exist, however, and the question from a dentist in Chicago is an example. He owns some unusual Papua stamps in the first airmail series; his stamps have grey tones in the borders and he wondered if they were varieties or if the colours had changed by sunlight or gases.

The dentist's question and others like it cannot be answered under normal circumstances from books, not even the specialized handbooks. A good means of getting technical answers is to locate a specialist in the country or subject. Most philatelists gladly share their knowledge.

The first airmail stamps of Papua were overprinted issues on 1916 ordinary stamps printed by John Ash who used snowy white paper; by J.B. Cooke who used creamy-toned paper, and by T.S. Harrison who used a deep cream-coloured paper. All three printers made the stamps with bright blue-green borders. Therefore, the colour in the dentist's Papua stamps must have been artificially changed by sunlight or some chemical. The normal stamps do not exist with grey tones in the borders.

And so the endless rounds of questions and answers keep the world of stamp collecting an ever-changing one. Little wonder that so many millions of people collect postage stamps.

11

PRACTICAL SUGGESTIONS

Publilius Syrus, the Syrian first-century Latin writer, said: "Many receive advice, few profit from it." These words from a wise man more than 2000 years ago remain sound today. Every Stamp Bug who starts collecting needs help and advice and should never be disturbed by small problems. They fade away one by one as collecting opens a new world for every person who enters the hobby.

Sammy Rotenberg, who said he was ten, wrote to ask about stamps of Israel as an investment. Sam received wrong advice from his father who had years of experience in the grain exchange in Chicago, but knew nothing about stamps or postage stamp collecting. After his father advised him to invest in Israeli stamps, Sam went to a stamp dealer in the Loop area of the city and bought a $2 package of low-denomination Israeli stamps. About a year later Rotenberg senior wrote a scathing letter condemning

stamp collecting because his son's expenditure had not risen to $25.

Several lessons come from this example. Stamp Bugs, especially beginners, should not buy stamps as an investment. Mothers and fathers never buy dolls or hockey skates for their children hoping to sell them a year later for twice their original cost. Parents buy these toys for the pleasure their children get from them. Stamps can bring the same pleasure.

The second mistake Sammy made occurred when he received advice from his father who knew nothing about postage stamps. Parents who hope to help their children can get assistance from experienced collectors. Experienced collectors may be found by asking dealers or post office clerks.

Sam's third mistake was the purchase of postage stamps from a single country. No beginner can possibly know which stamps to collect when he confines himself to one country. He also said in one letter that he did not own a book or catalogue of Israeli stamps. Every collector needs stamp books to help learn about the hobby or else his progress will be slowed.

What Are Philatelic Agencies?

Philatelic Agencies are in post office departments in most parts of the world. Originally their main service catered to stamp dealers everywhere who bought stamps in quantities for resale to their stamp collecting customers. Some agencies still deal with dealers exclusively and will not sell their stamps to individual collectors. Most countries, however, will service private accounts, but they put obstacles in the way of the customers they hope to obtain. Here are the necessary steps you should take to get stamps from agencies:

1.   Write for a list of stamps available. The cost is about 35c for postage both ways. Wait a month or two for the list.
2.   Select the stamps you need, then go to a bank or post office and buy a money order or post office order. Put the money order in your envelope and pay for the postage at a total cost of 50c or so for postage and fees.
3.   Wait again for your stamps to arrive in perhaps six to eight weeks and hope for good stamps.
4.   By now you have spent nearly one dollar on postage and fees and you wasted about four months. You could go to a stamp dealer, select your wants and pay for them all in a few hours including travel time. Or you can write to a stamp dealer stating which stamps you need and get them within a week or two.

Conclusion: Young or beginner Stamp Bugs should not buy stamps from philatelic agencies owing to the high costs, lengthy delays and possible disappointments. The following is an example of a woman who would not take this advice.

Some time ago a listener from southern Alberta wrote to the CBC Stamp Club and started a correspondence that lasted about four years. She said that she was a beginner and wanted the address of a western European philatelic agency. For two years she continued her barrage of letters on the same topic — cheap stamps from this philatelic agency.

She didn't know that for several reasons beginners should never buy stamps from the agencies of foreign countries. But she paid no attention and wrote to the address she got from the radio program. About a year later she wrote again and blamed us for the damaged stamps she received from the philatelic agency. Six months later she changed her tone when the agency replaced her damaged stamps. Nonetheless she continued her letters for another six months, then ended her correspondence, now convinced she had made a serious mistake.

Beginners: Take Care

A beginning Stamp Bug, regardless of his age, is bound to make some mistakes; a boy or girl of eight can make the same mistakes as an adult of fifty. And they ask the same questions. Therefore, a few suggestions to beginners may save them time, money, and frustration.

Never remove a stamp from its cover without first determining whether it is more valuable on its cover. Some non-collectors in Southampton, Ontario, received two envelopes through the mail in the fall of 1959. They threw one in the garbage, and they carelessly steamed the stamp off the other. They had bought two others at the local post office, but had not used them. All four stamps were the Canadian St. Lawrence Seaway two-colour inverts, accidentally sold as normal ones.

These were rare stamps printed by error with one part of the design upside down. Through lack of knowledge, the owners made a serious mistake in removing the stamps from the envelopes. They sold their rarities for $2500; if the stamps had been left on their covers they would have been worth $4000 at that time.

Beginners often destroy good stamps by handling them carelessly. A woman in southern Ontario had acquired her husband's stamp collection and proceeded to remount part of it. She carefully arranged the Canadian mint series of 1897 complete from half-cent to $5 and mounted each stamp with a strip of cellulose tape over the face and a half inch on each side of the album page. In this way she partly destroyed those scarce stamps. While this tape will come off if the stamps are soaked in water for an hour or so, the water in that time will also remove the gum. And if the gum is missing, the stamps become unused stamps — doubtful status that suggests the stamps may have been used but not cancelled. Experienced collectors avoid such material.

Collectors often lose time in trying to remove stamps by steaming. Soaking stamps off paper is better than steaming because many stamps can be soaked at one time. If one wants to remove a stamp that is stuck on an album page, sometimes one must make a choice between losing an album page or the stamps, or on some rare occasions choosing between the loss of a wallet and the stamps if any stamps are stuck in a wallet.

Postage stamps for collections should not be transported in wallets that are carried in pockets near a person's body. These stamps may crease or if they are mint they may stick to part of the wallet. A man in Winnipeg partly destroyed a Canadian St. Lawrence Seaway invert in his wallet. Any effort in restoration of damaged postage stamps is time lost through lack of forethought or knowledge.

Books on stamp collecting are available in public libraries; collectors should borrow them and read them carefully to save time, money, and frustration.

Auctions Are Not For Beginners

Young Kenneth Manning, a junior Stamp Bug, decided to attend a postage stamp auction. After all he had been collecting stamps for six years, and he was eighteen by that time. Numerous collectors in the hobby for that many years believe they know everything there is to know about philately. And Ken admits he was no exception. Before he went, his father called the auctioneer to guarantee payment for anything that Ken might buy.

The auctioneer began with a list of prestamp covers.* Ken found these dull, but the auctioneer worked so fast the young man had difficulty keeping up to the bids. Although he had no previous thoughts on what he would buy, he fancied some of the Italian States issues. The auctioneer started one lot at 275 with quick increases to 325,

* Letters mailed before adhesive postage stamps were introduced on May 6, 1840. Letters sent without postage stamps after they had been issued, but before the use of adhesive stamps was made compulsory in countries throughout the world, have a different name: they are stampless covers. Possibly a majority of stamp collectors incorrectly call both prestamp and stampless covers by the same name — that is stampless covers.

350, 425 and at 450 Ken held up his hand so that every person in the room could see him. But the bidding continued to $475 and the issues were quickly sold for $500. What a relief. Ken suddenly woke up to find he had bid $450, not $4.50. He didn't go to another postage stamp sale for ten years.

Mint Stamps or Used?

Ever since people began collecting stamps more than a hundred years ago, they have asked dealers and friends about a choice between used and mint stamps. Evidently the answer will never be found to the satisfaction of everyone. Many collectors prefer one to the other, while some try to collect both. All put forth sound arguments for their choice.

Mint stamps are stamps that have never been cancelled and still bear their original gum, just as they came from the printers. Mint stamps offer a kind of beauty in their pristine condition. Some collectors argue that postmarks, regardless of their light cancels, reduce the perfection of the stamps and often lower their commercial value.

Many used stamps, especially some of the early British colonials, command much higher prices than mint ones; the stamps of Heligoland, for example. Stamps of Papua issued before 1932 are at least ten times as scarce used as they are mint.

Postage stamps used on their original covers may be a hundred times as scarce as the same stamps in mint condition. The first stamps used in British New Guinea — later called Papua — do not exist mint. The first stamps were a Queensland issue, cancelled N.G. (for New Guinea).

Prior to 1900 some collectors preferred used stamps because they thought certain mint issues could be low-value reprints or government imitations. Modern collectors do not have such apprehensions. Reprinted stamps seem to be a thing of the past.

Some of the classical stamps, usually classified by their dates of issue before 1870, virtually do not exist in mint condition; for example, the stamps of the Bermuda Perot issues, the embossed stamps of Natal, 1857, or the 1850-1 issue of British Guiana.

Certain modern collectors invest in postage stamps rather than real estate or stocks and bonds. Apparently this hoarding began after the First World War, when European currencies, bonds, and real estate all fluctuated beyond safe investment levels. These people sought mint stamps, but they never mounted them with hinges. The fad of mint-never-hinged began. Today it has gone beyond the control of dealers and suppliers. One man recently sought a used stamp never hinged, an utterly ridiculous request, because one could easily soak a hinge from a stamp and leave no trace of the hinge.

Fortunately for philately, the mint-never-hinged people rarely contribute anything worthwhile to the hobby. They do not belong to serious philatelic clubs, write about stamps for philatelic papers, or exhibit. They just bury themselves in the postage stamp investments and long for next year's stamp catalogues to see how much they made in some imaginary transactions.

Mint postage stamps are invariably more fragile than used issues. Because they can easily become stuck together, especially in humid climates, they must be stored with the greatest care.

Should a person collect mint or used? That remains a personal choice. There is no guiding rule, but the beginning Stamp Bug should remember that mint stamps are fragile and most difficult to preserve in superb quality. Used stamps are much easier to preserve.

12

FOR ADVANCED STAMP BUGS

Stamp Catalogues

Curiosity is one valuable characteristic of Stamp Bugs. They take great delight in discovering all there is to know about the stamps they collect. When they entered the hobby, geography played an important part in satisfying a variety of curiosities. And as they extend their collecting activities, that curiosity takes new forms. One of them is the postage stamp catalogue. The catalogue opens a new world to advancing Stamp Bugs. The prices of each stamp unused and used are merely a part of the broad range of information these books contain. Headings on the lists tell perforation sizes and kinds of paper, such as wove, laid, pelure, and other less common varieties.

A page from a Scott's stamp catalogue illustrates the details available on one issue: it shows a stamp illustration and description of the design. The A226 is the number of the design, not the catalogue number. This stamp was issued in 1967 on April 28. It was engraved and perforated (Perf.) 12. Number 469 is Scott's Part One Catalogue number. A226 refers to the design number above, and then the 5c blue & red describes the colours and denomination of the stamp. The text in small letters below the stamp tells that the stamp was issued to commemorate the Canadian exposition, EXPO 67, the International Exhibition held in Montreal from April 28 until October 27, 1967.

Every stamp catalogue is different, but the basic ideas are similar. They illustrate at least one stamp in a series and give it a number, type or a letter with a number. The numbers in the left columns are the catalogue numbers that are varied from one publication to another. The descriptions of denominations, colours, perforation sizes, types of paper: wove, laid, watermarked or others are given as well. When watermarks appear in stamps, the editors usually describe them by numbers.

Most catalogues have instructions for their use in the front, and by following the directions even junior Stamp Bugs can learn how to use the catalogues. A person should learn how to use stamp catalogues. These books contain a wealth of information besides the lists of prices, and if collectors use them wisely they can be valuable reference books. But good advice is to "persist until you master them." David Doyle, the television actor, said, "Winners never quit . . . quitters never win."

1967, Apr. 28 Engraved Perf. 12
469   A226   5c blue & red   20   5
Issued to commemorate EXPO '67, International Exhibition, Montreal, Apr. 28–Oct. 27, 1967.

Extract from a stamp catalogue

Kinds of Stamps

Stamp collecting opens many doors to future types of education in virtually every field of human endeavour. Reading books,

asking questions, and talking to experienced collectors all help in the quest for knowledge, but sometimes mistakes appear in books that are considered to be accurate. For example, to the question "What is a postage stamp?" one established dictionary quotation reads: an official stamp affixed to mail matter as a sign that the postage has been paid.

This definition is wrong in the word *official*. The people do not use official stamps because in the countries that had them government members or government departments used them. The word should have been *authorized*. Official stamps are one of more than a hundred different kinds of postage stamps. The most common kinds are regular issues that continue in use for a long period of time, some more than twenty-five years. The collectors call these *definitive stamps*. Post offices order them time and time again as supplies run low.

Commemorative Stamps are issued to mark some event or to honour well-known people who made numerous contributions of value to their own people or to people of the world.

Bermuda stamp to commemorate the Olympic Games in 1964

Special Issues often resemble commemoratives in sizes and illustrations, but they do not honour people or events. They usually publicize appeals for animal

Handstruck postage due stamp from Ceylon

conservation, or the prevention of forest fires, or are issued as memorial stamps.

Mail carriers use *Postage Due Stamps* when the senders do not prepay enough postage on their mail. These postage due stamps also serve as receipts for the payment of postage after companies or organizations send envelopes bearing postal permits to mail back replies or donations without the addition of postage stamps. The permit holders pay the necessary fees to the post offices who send or give postage due stamps as receipts.

Canadian postage due stamp

Memorial Stamps, often printed in black, honour a person who died a few weeks or months earlier. Mourning stamps serve a

Memorial stamp for General Dwight D. Eisenhower which was issued Oct. 14, 1969.

Mourning stamp for Queen Astrid issued Dec. 1, 1935. Notice the black border.

similar purpose, but they are issued within days of the person's death. They have been printed with black frames around the portraits.

Airmail Stamps bear the name airmail or the equivalent words in the language of the country of origin: Par Avion or Poste aérienne in French; Lüftpost in German or Correo Aereo in Spanish.

Australian airmail stamp

Semi-Postal Stamps, often called "Charity Stamps" usually have two values shown on each stamp. One denomination is to prepay the postal charges, and the other, frequently indicated with a plus sign, is intended for a charity, a selected project, or research. Early semi-postals issued by the Australian state of Victoria did not have a surtax printed on the stamps but the one penny stamps sold

Semi-postal stamps show two values, one is the postal charge, the other is for charity.

for one shilling and the twopence half penny sold for two shillings six pence.

Booklet Stamps are small books of adhesive stamps produced by governments so that people can carry them and have stamps when they need them. Booklet stamps are usually sold in small panes of four to ten stamps, although some Canadian and French panes are longer. Canada issued small booklets of three stamps in a pane in the 1940s. Collectors save complete booklets or single panes complete with their tabs. They are the narrow bands of paper used to bind the panes in booklets.

Notice the tab at the left of this booklet pane.

Coil Stamps, sometimes called affixing machine stamps, are made in rolls from 100 to 1000 stamps for use in public vending machines or in office affixing machines. The meter postage stamp machines have replaced most of the office machines that used coil stamps.

Notice the straight edges at the top and bottom of these coil stamps.

Postal Tax Stamps do not pay for postal service. They raise funds for post office buildings, to maintain them or for other reasons. They must be used in the countries

Booklet pane from the Netherlands. The space at the left is used for advertisements.

that issue them, for example: Colombia, Cuba, Ecuador and the Dominican Republic.

 **This postal tax stamp was used to raise money for the post office.**

Henry Archer — Inventor

In stamp collecting, as in many other pursuits, one topic follows another. For example, postage stamps existed first and the means of separating them followed as a necessity. When Rowland Hill (later Sir Rowland Hill), the British postal reformer, introduced adhesive postage stamps in May, 1840, he had sheets of one-penny and two-pence stamps printed with margins around each stamp. However, there was no means of separating them. Postal workers had to snip them apart with scissors or cut them with sharp knives. Help came in October 1847 from an Irishman named Henry Archer.

Mr. Archer met with the Marquis of Clanricade, the Postmaster General of Great Britain, and told him about his invention of a machine to perforate stamps. He explained to the Postmaster, "I have contrived an inexpensive plan whereby the postage stamps may be detached from the sheet." After years of experiments and the development of his invention, he received £4000 from the British Treasury Department for his perforating machine and patents. On Jan. 28, 1854 British postage stamps "perforated 16" went on sale to the public. Countries everywhere followed the British lead.

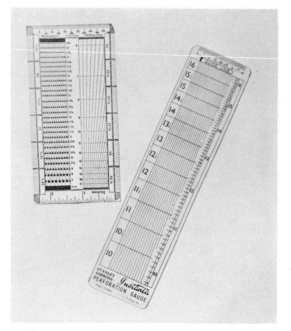

Perforation gauges

The number of perforations in a given space varies; some perforations are fine, others coarse. The standard used to gauge perforations is two centimetres. Thus "perforation 15" (or perf 15 or p.15) means that there are fifteen holes in a space of two centimetres around the edges of a stamp. All four sides of a stamp must be considered when perforations are measured. All four sides are often perforated in the same gauge, but two perforation sizes in one stamp are also common, and some have three or even four sizes of perforation.

Perforations are described as follows:

— Perf or p. 12 means perforated 12 all around;

— Perf or p. 12 x 8 means perforated 12 on top and bottom and 8 on both sides.

The first figure always indicates the top and bottom, the second, the sides. Further compound perforations are recorded in a clockwise manner: top, right side, bottom, and left side.

The perforation gauge is a rectangle of card, plastic or metal, usually printed with rows of black dots of different sizes in a column. Sometimes the stamps are measured in the centre of the gauge, while the rows of dots on the edges are used to determine perforation sizes of mounted stamps.

A stamp is placed on the column scale and moved up and down until the correct row of dots exactly corresponds to the perforation on the stamp. The perf number can then be read.

Above you can see various types of magnifiers for viewing details of stamps. From left to right their strengths are: 4 power, 50 power, 10 power, and 20 power.

Blind Perforations Require A Magnifier

Bob Murphy must have been flying high as a jet the day he wrote about his find of a rarity. He discovered a partly perforated stamp from the United States. When he sent the stamp for examination it was a perfect example of blind perforations.

When the perforating pins strike the paper but do not cut through it, they leave impressed circles where the perforations should be. These are called blind perforations. The illustration of the U.S. stamp is such an excellent example that the engravers of the printing plates were forced to procure an enlarged photograph, and then have it retouched to indicate the locations of the lines of perforations. From the front the stamp seems to be an imperforate stamp from the right side of the pane.

Stamps with blind perforations are sometimes mistaken at first for imperforate varieties. Other stamps with some blind perfs tear from the sheet unevenly. When only some of the perfs are blind and adjacent portions are normal on the same stamp, collectors say that the stamps have rough perforations.

Rouletting

During Henry Archer's years of experiments with stamp perforations he worked on a system of making slits in the margins of stamps without punching holes in the paper. Rouletting is the name of these nine different types of separations all noted in postage stamp catalogues:

Arc roulette — nearly microscopic semi-circles that are sometimes called serrated roulettes.

Archer roulettes — wavy lines.

Line roulette — straight lines.

Line roulette in colour — lines with printing in the colours of the stamps.

Pin roulette or Zigzag roulette — a series of pin holes.

Rhomboid roulette — a series of diamond shaped cuts. They are also known as double pointed tooth roulettes.

Saw tooth roulette — single stamps resemble perforated stamps with pointed teeth.

Serpentine roulette — wavy lines creating large hills and valleys or the movements of a snake that suggest the name. Finland used these.

Diamond or Lozenge roulette — the rarest of all roulettes used by Madeira.

Rough perforations — often resemble roulettes of uncertain types, quite common among certain stamps of Brazil and New Zealand.

Notice the margin on the bottom of the stamp with the roulettes (wavy lines) about 1/8" from the bottom.

This roulette has slits but no holes in the margins, and the roulette is all around the stamp.

Susse perforations — resemble the serpentine roulettes of Finland. The Susse Brothers of Paris invented a machine to perforate fifty stamps at one time, but when they did not get a contract from the French post office they sold the machine to a stamp dealer in Paris.

Stamp collectors should not feel disappointed if they have difficulties trying to identify the various types of roulettes. While the roulettes were a means of separating stamps mainly before 1900, South Africa during the Second World War issued small postage stamps perforated around pairs and strips of three and rouletted horizontally or vertically between each stamp. Catalogues explain the details and sizes of both perforations and roulettes.

Advanced Accessories

As stamp collectors advance they acquire more accessories, gadgets, and instruments to help them. Apart from watermark trays, albums, hinges, and the tongs that beginners require, a few other instruments are useful.

Electric watermark detectors are battery powered with a strong light that shines through the stamps and show watermarks of all kinds, including the lines in laid papers, the heavy batons in batonne paper, or the squares visible in quadrille papers. Collectors must learn how to use the electric watermark detectors and the colour filters that come with them. They have instruction sheets in each package.

Black light makes the fluorescence,

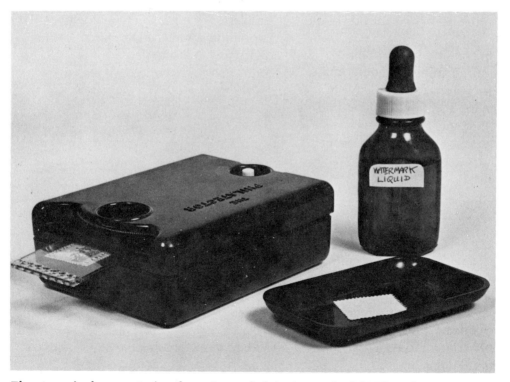

The stamp is shown entering the watermark detector on the left. The other implements can be used if you don't have a detector. Put the watermark liquid in the tray and the watermarks will show up.

luminescence or phosphorescence glow in the dark. Any person who starts a collection of tagged or chemically treated stamps needs black light so that he can see the tagging chemical that glows under the black light.

Black light lamp

The letter in plain light

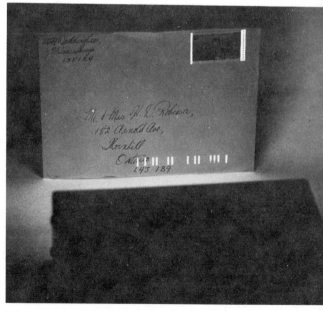

The letter under black light shows the postal code and tagging, but not the stamp.

The stamp press, like the electric watermark detector, is a fun gadget that may be useful, but stamp collectors do not need them. A heavy book placed over drying papers can press stamps nearly as well as the stamp press. The press is a pair of aluminum plates about three by five inches supported at each end by solid posts and a dozen pieces of cardboard in the same size as the top and bottom plates. A hand screw forces the plates together. Stamps placed between the cardboard sheets for an hour come out wrinkle free, but the press will not remove a crease.

Micrometers are the only means of determining the exact thickness of papers, yet stamp collectors seem to neglect them. According to Roger Nixon, a pulp and paper executive, people cannot distinguish between two papers with a difference of

1000th of an inch in thickness. Despite this fact, catalogue editors refer to thick and thin papers. But exactly how thick is thick and how thin is thin?

In the studies of most postage stamps, the precise thickness of papers has no bearing on the results, but with other projects the micrometers are imperative. The first twenty-eight stamps from British New Guinea (1901-5) listed in *Gibbons British Commonwealth Edition* catalogue were issued on thick and thin papers with horizontal and vertical watermarks. A check of papers that lasted over ten years with more than 1000 stamps issued in these years revealed a wide range of thickness varieties. The thin stamps measured from two and three-quarter thousandths of an inch to three-and-a-half thousandths. Measured on the micrometer those figures read: .00275

Stamp Press

and .0035. The thick stamps in the same series measure from four to six thousandths. Micrometers can be fun instruments and profitable too when they uncover scarce paper varieties.

Printing

Most postage stamps have been printed by four different processes: steel engraving, gravure, lithography and letterpress.

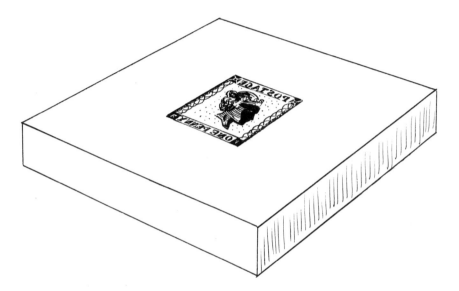

ILLUSTRATING THE ORIGINAL DIE, ENGRAVED IN REVERSE. IT IS FROM THIS "HARDENED" DIE, THAT IMPRESSIONS ARE TAKEN BY THE TRANSFER ROLLER.

A — B

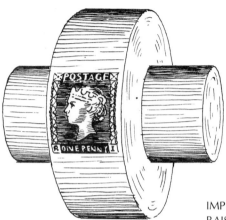

IMPRESSION OF A TRANSFER ROLLER WITH THE DESIGN
RAISED ON THE SURFACE. WHEN THE TRANSFER ROLLER
IS ROCKED OVER THE SOFT STEEL PLATE, THE DESIGN
ENTERS THE PLATE IN REVERSE.

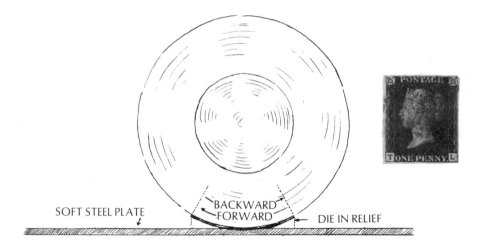

DIAGRAM SHOWING TRANSFER ROLLER ROCKING A DESIGN
INTO THE SOFT STEEL PLATE. IT IS DURING THIS OPERATION
THAT RE-ENTRIES AND TRANSFER SHIFTS USUALLY OCCUR.

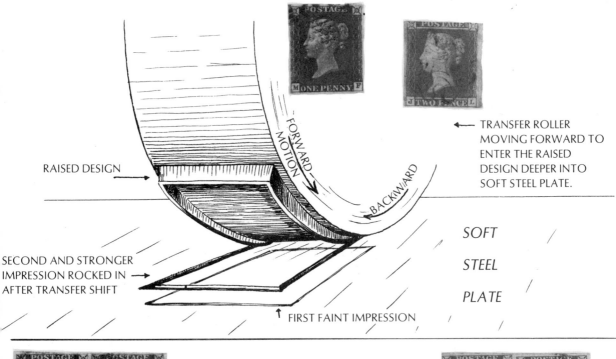

RAISED DESIGN →

FORWARD MOTION

BACKWARD

← TRANSFER ROLLER MOVING FORWARD TO ENTER THE RAISED DESIGN DEEPER INTO SOFT STEEL PLATE.

SOFT

STEEL

PLATE

SECOND AND STRONGER IMPRESSION ROCKED IN AFTER TRANSFER SHIFT →

↑ FIRST FAINT IMPRESSION

A TRANSFER ROLLER ROCKING THE DESIGN INTO THE PLATE. THIS ILLUSTRATION SHOWS A TRANSFER SHIFT. (THE FIRST FAINT IMPRESSION.)

Steel engraving

Steel engraving, by far the most important postage stamp printing process, is the only nearly forgery proof method of printing stamps. Steel engraved printing plates require more time to manufacture than do other plates, and they cost more. The following drawings by George Deer were developed from sketches made at the big postage stamp show held in September, 1951 at the exhibition grounds in Toronto.

Gravure printing

Gravure printing in the past twenty years or more has made possible the distinctively shiny postage stamps that are like pictures in a mail order catalogue. The usual snow-white paper used for gravure printed stamps makes them look different from other stamps mounted on an album page.

Like steel engraving, gravure printing is an intaglio process. The printing medium consists of lines or dots, cut, etched or engraved below the surface of the plates.

The gravure printing method shows a photographic likeness of the subject reproduced because photography plays such an important part in the process of making the plates. The subjects for reproduction are photographed, then positives are made on glass from a negative or negatives. The solid masses in the original must be reproduced as solid masses in the finished printing and the light tones must also be made light.

When graduating tones are reproduced by gravure they must be broken into small, nearly microscopic, square cells. The plate makers follow predetermined steps, including the application of carbon tissue, a gelatin substance, to copper printing plates. Finally, the plates are treated with etching solutions of various strengths that bite through the gelatin to create every kind of pocket from the shallowest to the deepest. These tiny cups hold ink that is transferred to the paper to produce the images like the original art work.

Lithography

The term lithography originated years ago when printing was done from smooth pieces of flat stones. The word lithography comes from the Greek — *lithos* means stone and *graphein* means to write. The original lithographic principle is based on the fact that grease and water do not mix. In this kind of lithographic plate making, the image to be printed is affixed to the surface of the plate by a thin film of greasy ink. Water on the plate repels the grease.

The grease image on the plates can be drawn by hand, made by photographic means, or can be made by transfers from a master plate or stone.

The increasing demand for lithographic stone caused a shortage of the finest products. A substitute material became necessary and as a result zinc and aluminum metallic plates came into use. Today most lithographers use metallic plates. Since these metal plates are thin, they can be used on rotary printing cylinders. Two types of lithography may result: one prints directly on the paper while the other method, called offset lithography, prints the impressions on a rubber blanket covering a cylinder. From there the ink is offset to the paper. Lithographic presses have two sets of rollers, one for ink and the other for water.

Letterpress

For over a hundred years stamp catalogue editors have called letterpress printing by wrong names. The Scott editors use the words "typography" or "typographed" (typo), which refers to the appearance or arrangement of printed matter. Gibbons' editors use the terms "surface printed" and "typographed," but never "letterpress printed."

Letterpress printing is always produced from relief printing surfaces like the lines on fingers, or the type of cash register tapes. When a printing surface is in relief the spaces between the printing areas are lower and do not print because they do not come in contact with the paper. Of all the printing plates used to make postage stamps, letterpress plates are the fastest and most economical to produce.

Engravers make two kinds of letterpress printing plates used for printing stamps: halftone and line. Sometimes they combine the two. The purpose of the engraving is to transfer an image to a metal plate so that a reproduction of the original copy may be printed.

A special photographic printing method applies the image to the surface of a metal plate that is to be etched. When this print is completed, it acts like an acid-proof covering on all printing areas of the image. But owing to the way this part of the process works, all of the non-printing areas, like the spaces between the lines, dots, and other parts of the image, are left without a protective covering. The etching acid therefore bites into them deep enough to prevent contact with the paper when the upper areas are inked and printed.

Stamp Papers

Postage stamps have been printed on numerous materials including silk, foil, and cardboard, but the most common material is paper. It comes in many sizes, colours, textures, and degrees of thickness. It has been made by hand and machine, and from many substances, such as flax, papyrus, cloth, and most commonly, wood pulp. Paper is especially interesting to stamp collectors because the rarity of some postage stamps varies with the type of paper the printers used. Just two of the Canadian 1868 two-cent stamps are known to have been printed on a type of paper known as laid paper. A knowledge of paper often helps in the detection of scarce or rare stamps. Yet even many advanced students of stamps lack a knowledge of paper manufacture and how stamps are produced.

More than fifty kinds of paper have been used for stamps. Here are some of the common kinds:

— *Wove paper,* a general term for papers that are not of the laid type. Wove refers to the imprint or impressions left on the surface of the paper by the woven wire on which the paper is made.

— *Laid paper* was originally made by hand before machines were invented to manufacture paper. The earlier paper makers, mainly before 1830, used frames to hold the mixture of fibres and other materials that formed in sheets the size of their frames. When the wire screens were made with laid mould wires, the results were laid papers with alternating thick and thin variations in the paper substance. These lines may be seen as light and darker lines when the paper is held to light. The modern laid papers are produced by bits soldered on the dandy-roll on the paper machine.

— *Watermarked paper,* a common type used for stamp production to help prevent forgery. The watermarks consist of letters, numerals, designs such as flowers, umbrellas, pineapples, and others, as well as combinations of these, or an overall pattern in lines, squares, diagonals, or batons. They can often be seen by holding the paper to light or with a watermark detector.

— *Hard, soft, or porous papers* are general terms that are usually used in comparing one paper with another. Beginners may study these types by consulting papermaking books. Collectors may buy known varieties for comparison with other stamps. Little or no help seems available in books about stamp collecting.

— *Batonné paper* can be either wove or laid with parallel watermarked straight lines farther apart than those in laid paper; in laid batonné, both types can

Wove

Laid

Batonne

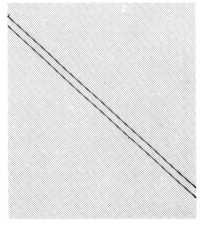

Quadrille

Dickinson

Granite

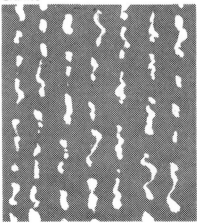

Courtesy: Scott Publishing Co. New York City

be seen by holding the stamps to light or by watermark tests.

— *Chalky paper* is a patented paper made with a chalk coating as a security measure to help prevent forgery and to prohibit people from erasing postmarks. Collectors are warned to handle chalky paper stamps with care, as the delicate surface often runs or floats off when the stamps are submerged in water. It has been used for some British and British colonial stamps since 1902.

— *Cowan papers* usually have a closely woven appearance, with watermarks often difficult to see with any degree of clarity. Some stamps of New Zealand show examples of this paper.

— *De La Rue paper* is a special paper invented by the security printers and used for postage stamp printing. It is used in many New Zealand stamps; the paper is never extra thick and curls easily from top to bottom. Often the gums used on stamps influence this curling.

— *Pelure papers* are so thin that the stamp designs may be seen from the back. There are both wove or laid pelure papers.

— *Joined papers* are usually stamps that have been separated from strips, then glued together in rolls. In the earliest coils the joints, or joined paper pairs or strips, were more common because the printers made the stamps in sheets, cut them into strips then glued the strips together to make a continuous roll of 500, 1000, or more. On some occasions papers in rolls (web paper) have been joined to connect one roll to the preceding one. Usually the resulting stamps are discarded in the printer's waste basket. Joined stamps of this nature found in panes are quite scarce, but they should not command excessive prices, probably not more than double the price of normal stamps.

— *Chemically treated papers* are a comparatively modern development. The paper is treated with chemicals to make it glow under black light and was designed for use in automatic sorting machines all over the world. Some of the recent stamps of Australia, Germany, and the Netherlands glow beautifully under black light, yet show nothing under ordinary daylight. These modern papers are divided into two classes: fluorescent papers, made with chemicals in the paper substance itself, and phosphorescent papers, with the materials added to the stamps. The current Canadian low-value stamps fall into this classification. Some are tagged stamps with phosphorescent material in stripes or bands across the face of the stamp.

— *Safety papers* are any papers specially made or treated to prevent forgery. There have been many interesting types — for example, the three kinds containing silk threads. One is Dickinson paper, containing silk threads. Another has tiny coloured threads in small pieces spread throughout the paper. The third type, granite or silurian paper, contains threads so small that they can hardly be seen.

In 1866, Prussia used a unique type with an odd name, goldbeater's skin. Prussia had the stamp design printed on the back of each stamp; this paper was so transparent that the design showed through to the front. These are probably among the ten most fragile stamps ever issued by a postal authority.

— *Winchester paper* is a brand name of a security paper made with a decorative surface of semi-circles printed row on row in greyish-blue, rather like cheque paper. The name Winchester appears in a rhomboid or decorative frame. This surface design prevents the stamps from being cleaned and used a second time. Venezuela used Winchester paper from the 1932-8 regular issue stamps and the 1932 airmail stamps.

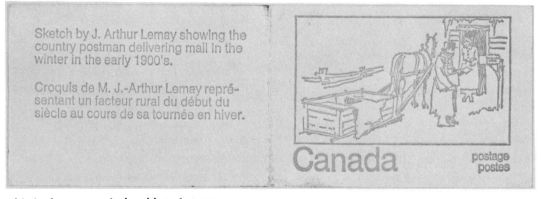

This is the cover of a booklet of stamps.

Afghanistan

Austria

Bantam-size

Belgium

Bosnia and Herzegovina

Bulgaria

China

Postal Tax (Colombia)

Crete

Denmark

Danish West Indies

Netherlands Indies

Egypt

Finland

French Colonies

Great Britain

Greece

Hungary

Ireland

Israel

Japan

Morocco

Moiré
Overprint
See Glossary

Norway

Palestine

Prussia

Persia
(now Iran)

Russia

San Marino	Serbia	Siam (now Thailand)	Spain

Switzerland	Sweden

Transvaal	Turkey

Venezuela	Wurttemberg

GLOSSARY

A list of names and terms to help collectors of all ages.

This is not a check list; the examples are chosen at will and do not represent all the stamps that fall under each classification.

A

ACORES   Azores.

adhesive stamps   the kind sold with gum on the back ready to stick on mail.

AFGHAN, AFGHANES   Afghanistan.

AFRICA OCCIDENTAL ESPANOLA   Spanish West Africa.

AFRICA ORIENTALE ITALIANA   Italian East Africa.

AFRIQUE EQUATORIALE GABON   Gabon.

AFRIQUE OCCIDENTALE FRANÇAISE   French West Africa.

ALGERIE   Algeria.

AMTLICHER VERKEHR   Wurttemberg.

apercevoir   Canada, Belgium, France and many French Colonies. Postage due stamps.

A PAYER TE BETALEN   postage due stamps of Belgium since 1870.

auction   sales held to dispose of postage stamps and other philatelic items such as covers or entire collections. Auctioneers prepare catalogues listing all items and send them to collectors on their lists. Sales are held mainly in two ways: entirely by mail (mail auctions) and in front of a room full of buyers (called the floor) and from mail bidders who use the same catalogues.

aur   (Insc.) coins of Iceland. 100 aurar equal one rigsdaler. Singular is eyrir.

avisporto   Denmark. Newspaper stamps, 1907-15.

AZERBAIDJAN   Azerbaijan

B

BAHRAIN (ovpt.)   on stamps of India, Bahrain.

Bani   (coin) overprinted on stamps of Austria, Romania under Austrian occupation. also inscribed on Romanian stamps.

BAYERN, BAYR   Bavaria.

B. DPTO. ZELAYA   Nicaragua, Province of Zelaya.

BELGIE (insc.) on stamps of Belgium.

BELGIEN (ovpt.)   on German stamps, Belgium under German Occupation.

BELGISCH CONGO (insc.) on stamps of Belgian Congo.

bicentennial   the 200th anniversary of some event of importance to a country or the birth or death of a prominent citizen. Stamps often commemorate bicentennials.

bicoloured   any stamp printed in two colours. (see multicoloured).

bilingual stamps   those printed in two languages. Examples: Canada, South Africa, Belgium and others. UN postage stamps bear five languages.

bisected stamps   or bisects are stamps cut in half diagonally, vertically or horizontally to provide stamps for the correct rates of postage. Usually made during the shortages of certain stamps that would pay the correct rates. Stamps cut in other portions are called, "split stamps."

Bisect

Bishop Marks   Henry Bishop invented postmarks about 1661 when King Charles II of England rented the postal service to him for seven years. After people blamed Bishop for holding their letters, he developed small circular marks with numerals for the date plus short forms for months. He struck one on each letter when he received it.

block   three or more stamps from two or more horizontal rows. They do not have to be in square or rectangular even units as older stamp collectors believed.

BOFTGEBIET   overprinted on stamps of Germany, Lithuania.

bogus labels   often called stamps by error. These items were never issued by any government and could not pay for postal service.

BOHMEN UND MAHREN   (Insc.) Bohemia and Moravia in Czechoslovakia, issued stamps 1939-44.

BOLLO POSTALE   San Marino.

booklet stamps   those in small panes from 3 to 25 stamps or more bound in card or paper covers either sewn or stapled together.

BOSNIEN-HERZEGOVINA   Bosnia and Herzegovina.

BRASIL   Brazil.

BRITISH CONSULAR MAIL   Madagascar, issued by British Consulate.

BRITISH NEW GUINEA   Papua.

BRITISH SO. AFRICA COMPANY   Rhodesia, when overprinted B.C.A. British Central Africa.

briefpost   Germany under French Occupation.

BUITEN BEZIT (ovpt.)   Dutch Indies.

BULGARIE   Bulgaria.

BURMA (ovpt.)   on stamps of India, Burma.

C

CABO (ovpt.)   Nicaragua — Cabo Gracias a Dios, "Cape Thanks To God," a cape in the northeast corner of Nicaragua.

**Nicaragua,
Cabo Gracias a Dios**

CAHATOPHyMb   Bulgaria.

CAMB AUST. SIGILLUM NOV   New South Wales.

cancellations   defacing marks, cuts or punctures made to prevent the stamps from being used a second time. Cancels include pen and ink crosses or lines (pen cancels) or written letters, dates, initials or names (manuscript cancels). Afghanistan cancelled early stamps by a pie-shape cut in each adhesive postage stamp. Spain punctured some postage stamps with circular holes. Stamps often sold with printed cancels are called pre-cancelled stamps.

catalogue value   the price listed in a postage stamp catalogue for each stamp. Specialized catalogues often price covers with or without adhesive stamps, postal markings and first-day covers.

CCCP (abbr.)   for Union of Socialist Soviet Republic, Russia.

c. de pesos   Philippines.

CECHY A MORAVA   Czechoslovakia, Czechia (Bohemia) and Moravia.

Cello-paq   name of Canadian postage stamp packages sold in two miniature sheets of 25 of the two-cent and one sheet of 20 stamps in the five-cent value. These packs sold for $1 each.

CENTENAIRE DE L'ALGERIE   Algeria.

centesimi (coin)   Italy and Italian Colonies.

centimes (ovpt.)   on stamps of Germany, German Offices in Turkey.

centimes a percevoir   with numeral but no country name, Guadeloupe.

centimos   with no country name, Spain. Overprinted on stamps of France — Offices in Morocco.

CESKO-SLOVENSKO   Czechoslovakia.

CF (Fr. insc.)   on 1958 Human Rights Issue of French Equatorial Africa for use as the first issue of stamps for the Malagasy Republic. CF is French for Communauté française.

charity stamps   nickname for semi-postal stamps printed with two values and sold for the total of the two. Only part of the money pays for postal service while the smaller amount goes to some charity or predetermined objective.

chemins de fer spoorwegen   Belgium.

chessboard fashion   describes the stamp arrangement in sheets or panes so that any block of four contains two designs laid down with alternate stamps of the same design to resemble a checkerboard or chessboard pattern. Example: Algonkian Indians Canadian stamps of Nov. 28 1973.

chiffre taxe   with no country name given, on perforated stamps, France; on imperforate stamps, French Colonies.

CHINA (ovpt.)   on stamps of Hong Kong, Great Britain, Offices in China. On stamps of Germany, Offices in China.

CMS   complete matched set refers to plate number blocks of four stamps with the same plate numbers in all four positions: upper left and right, lower left and right. In U.S. stamps printed from flat plates, the numbers were most frequently in the top and bottom marginal paper. They were usually collected in blocks four in vertical-format stamps or six horizontal format stamps.

COCHIN, COCHIN ANCHAL   a feudatory state in India.

co-extensive lines   printed lines in short lengths around sheets and panes of stamps to protect the edges of the plates.

coil stamps   postage stamps in long strips originally made for use in vending machines. Great Britain and certain British colonies used stamps perforated on four sides but made in long strips for coil or roll postage. In other parts of the world coil stamps have

Coil stamps which have straight edges at the top and bottom

opposite sides or ends imperforate. Collectors save coil stamps in pairs or strips, rarely in singles.

colonies postes   French Colonies.

commemorative stamps   issues introduced to mark some event, anniversary or person.

COMORES   Grand Comoro Island.

COMPANHIA DE MOCAMBIQUE   Mozambique Co.

compound perforations   refers to two or more perforation sizes on one stamp. Two sizes are quite common but four are really scarce although some are found on the early stamps of Jugoslavia and on certain stamps in the 1906 pictorial series of Bosnia and Herzegovina.

comunicaciones   Spain.

correio   with no country name, Portugal.

correo or correspondencia urgente   Spain. Special delivery stamps.

counterfeit stamps   imitations of postage stamps. Two kinds have been made: to deceive the post office revenue or others for sale to the stamp collectors. Also known as forgeries. Not to be confused with bogus or faked stamps.

This counterfeit or forgery is the wrong size and has the wrong perforations.

correos y telegs   Spain.

CPbNJA or CPNCKA   Serbia.

CT., CTOT., CTOTNHKN (coins)   Bulgaria.

C.X.C. (abbr.)   for Serbs, Croats and Slovenes — Jugoslavia.

D

dandy roll   on a paper machine, the device that is a skeleton roll covered with woven wire riding on top of the wet sheet to give the upper surface of the paper the same wire markings as the lower surface of the paper that rests on the paper machine. The dandy roll also compresses the wet sheet and breaks up foam or air bubbles on the surface of the sheet. Laid markings and watermark designs are fastened to the dandy roll.

DANMARK   Denmark.

DEFICIT   Peru, postage due stamps.

definitive stamps   regular issues ordered from time to time. Other issues may be provisionals, special issues or commemorative stamps.

DEUTSCHE DEMOKRATISCHE REPUBLIK   Germany under Russian Occupation. (German Democratic Republic.) DDR.

DEUTSCHES REICH   Germany.

DEUTSCHE REICHS-POST   Germany.

DEUTSCHES REICH GENERALGOUVERNEMENT   Poland under German Occupation.

domestogrammes   name for Canadian postal stationery that combines a letter, envelope and stamp all in one. First issued on Oct. 17, 1973, they feature the floral emblems of Canadian provinces and territories.

doplata   Central Lithuania, Poland. Postage due stamps.

doplatit or doplatne   with no country name, postage due, Czechoslovakia.

DRZAVA (ovpt.)   1918 stamps of Jugoslavia or Yugoslavia, on 1910 stamps of Bosnia and Herzegovina.

dual purpose issue   stamps that were intended for use in two ways or for two or more events. Examples are postage and revenue stamps of Great Britain and some colonies. The Canadian 1973 commemorative stamps for the visit of Queen Elizabeth II and for the Commonwealth Heads of Government meeting Aug. 2 to 10, 1973. Stamps from souvenir sheets may serve as souvenirs of an event, entrance fees and for postage. Other examples are known.

E

E.C. dollars   East Caribbean money used in certain British West Indies islands, Antigua in 1973 is an example.

EE. UU. DE C.   Colombia, Tolima.

EGYPTE   Egypt.

EIRE or eiRe   Irish Free State known as Eire or Ireland.

ELWA (insc.)   1974 issue of Liberia features call letters of radio station in Monrovia; a station which continued to serve as the Voice of West Africa for 20 years.

EMPIRE FRANC   France.

error   a stamp with some mistake in it made by a workman or artist. Human beings create the errors while machines or equipment produce varieties. The word error had more glamor and possibility of higher prices than the term variety. Beware of varieties sold as errors. Many collectors and dealers do not know the difference.

ESCUELAS   (Span.) on Venezuela stamps 1879-82, and 1887. Revenues for school funds used for postage during shortages of regular stamps.

ESPANA   Spain.

ESTADO ESPANOL   Spanish State, Spain.

ETAT FRANCAIS (insc.)   France on June 7, 1943 issue of semi-postal stamps.

ETHIOPIA, ETHIOPIENNES   (Insc.) Ethiopia formerly called Abyssinia. A monarchy in Northeastern Africa.

E. U. DE COLOMBIA   United States of Colombia, Colombia.

F

fakes   genuine stamps altered to increase their value.

FEDERATED MALAY STATES   Straits Settlements, Federated Malay States.

feldpost   overprinted on stamps of Germany, German Military stamps.

fen, fn (coin)   Manchukuo. Fen as an overprint with Poczta Polska — Poland.

FILIPAS, FILIPINAS   Philippines.

filler (coin)   Hungary.

first day cover   a letter sheet, envelope or aerogram with adhesive or imprinted stamp or stamps cancelled on the day of issue. Mail from inaugural flights are called first-flight covers.

flugpost   airmail — Germany, Danzig, Austria.

forgery   see counterfeit.

franco bollo   with no country name given on perforated stamps — Italy.

FRANCO BOLLO DI STATO   (insc.) On official stamps of Italy, 1875. Also on newspaper stamps of 1862.

freaks   usually faulty production of stamps that should have been discarded as printers' waste. These abnormals are often badly perforated at any angle except through stamp margins. Others have been printed on the gum side. Other freaks exist. They are not errors unless their faults lie with a person, not a machine.

FREIMARKE   with no country name, Prussia. also printed on stamps of Bergedorf, Baden, Thurn and Taxis and on the early issues of Wurttemberg.

frimarke   Denmark, Norway, Sweden.

frimarke KGL post   Denmark.

FVERSTENTUM or FURSTENTUM LIECHTENSTEIN   Liechtenstein.

G

GENERAL GOUVERNEMENT   Poland after German conquest.

GRAND COMORE   Grand Comoro Islands.

GRAND LIBAN   Lebanon.

grills   embossed impressions, mainly in certain early U.S. stamps, to pick up the cancelling ink to prevent the stamps from being used a second time by removing the postal markings or cancels.

U.S.A. grill stamp

GRONLAND   Greenland.

gum   the adhesive substance on the back of stamps.

GUYANE FRANCAISE   French Guiana.

H

HAUT-SENEGAL-NIGER   Upper Senegal and Niger.

HEJAZ & NEJD, HEDJAZ & NEDJDE   Nejd, modern name is Saudi Arabia.

heller (coin)   Carinthia, Austria, Liechtenstein, Bosnia-Herzegovina.

HELVETIA   Switzerland.

HOBy   Montenegro.

HRVATSKA   Jugoslavia or Croatia.

I

I.E.F.   Indian Expeditionary Force — India.

IIOYTA   Russia.

IIOPTO MAPKA   Serbia.

IMPTO. DE GUERRA   Spain.

INDIA PORTUGUEZA   Portuguese India.

INDONESIA   Indonesia, formerly Dutch Indies.

I.O.M.   Isle of Man refers to stamps and

other philatelic items that some dealers advertise. This is not an official abbreviation.

inscription   usually the lettering on postage stamps and postal stationery items. Designs of heraldry or small units are often considered as inscriptions.

instruccion   Venezuela.

ISLAND   Iceland.

ITALIA, ITALIANE   Italy.

IRAN   Persia adopted Iran as its official name in 1935.

IRANIENNES, Iranien   Iran or Persia.

J

Jamaica   independent state formerly a British colony in the Caribbean Sea about 90 miles south of Cuba. First stamps used were British issues cancelled A-01 and others at later times. First colonial stamps issued on Nov. 23, 1860. (See *Gibbons British Commonwealth Edition* for details about British stamps used abroad.)

Japan   also inscribed Nippon (literally Great Japan) on some stamps. An empire in Eastern Asia, a monarchy under a new constitution of Nov. 3, 1946 in force on May 3, 1947. Island chain in the West Pacific off the east coast of Asia. Issued first stamps in April, 1871.

Java   one island in the Netherlands Indies used some former stamps overprinted Java in 1908.

joint pair   two stamps or panes of stamps pasted together to repair coils or make them into continuous rolls. Sheets or panes of stamps have been pasted together for

printing on the rotary presses to save time and work of threading a new roll through the presses. The joined parts are usually discarded. Do not separate joined stamps.

Jornaes   (insc.) on the newspaper stamps of Portugal.

Jour d'emission   French words in postmarks and cancels meaning day of issue. These cancellations are in Canadian first-day covers, usually from the capital city, Ottawa. They are used in some French and French-speaking colonial first-day covers. Some of the former French colonies now independent still use cancels — Jour d'emission.

JOURNAUX DAGBLADEN   overprinted on stamps of Belgium — Belgium. Newspaper stamps.

jubilee   normally a public festivity, but in stamp collecting, part of an event commemorating a person, place or special occasion. Stamps have been issued for the Silver Jubilee or the 25th anniversary of the reign of King George V. The Queen Victoria Golden Jubilee stamps of Great Britain (1887) marked the 50th year of Her Majesty's reign. In 1897 Canada issued a Diamond Jubilee set of stamps to honour Queen Victoria and the 60th year of her reign. Stamps mark other jubilees.

Jugoslavia   formerly the Kingdom of Serbs, Croats and Slovenes; also spelled Yugoslavia, the official name of the country since 1929. Republic in southeast Europe. Officially it is a federal people's republic comprising six federative republics or units: Bosnia and Herzegovina, Croatia, Macedonia, Montenegro, Serbia, and Slovenia. First stamps issued in 1918. (See stamp catalogues and encyclopedias for details.)

jump pair describes the different levels of stamps in roll postage commonly referred to as coil stamps. The roll stamps, especially Canadian, are made in the continuous strips on cylindrical presses that use curved plates. The jumps occur where the end of the plates make their last impression from the same plate as it turns on rotary presses, but does not fall on the same and exact level of the first impression. The jump pairs should not be separated since they take place about every 20th to 30th stamp according to the size of the plates. Jump pairs are much scarcer than other pairs in the same roll.

K

kap (coin) Latvia.

KENTTA-POSTI or KENTTA-POSTIA Finland Military Stamps.

keytypes a common design of postage stamps printed in large quantities usually for colonial postage. A second printing impressed the colonial name and denomination. Introduced as a means of reducing printing costs, Great Britain, Germany and Portugal used billions of keytype stamps for their colonies. France and Spain also used keytypes.

K.G.L. Denmark. On the early stamps 1851-68.

KGL/POST/FRM on early stamps of Denmark.

kina high value coin of Papua New Guinea introduced to replace the former dollar. A new series of five stamps issued on April 21, 1975 illustrates both the kina and the toea that replaced the former cent. (See toea.)

K.K. or KAISERLICHE KONIGLICHE OSTERREICHISCHE POST Imperial and Royal Austrian Post.

KOH, KOLL, KON (abbr.) Russian copek, unit of currency.

kop coin of Finland. 100 kopecks equal one ruble. Coinage changed in 1866 to: 100 pennia equal one markka.

KPAJbEBCTBO C. X. C. Jugoslavia.

KPALJEVSTVO (or KRALJEVINA) SRBA, HRVATA I SLOVENACA Kingdom of the Serbs, Croats and Slovenes — Jugoslavia.

KPHTH Crete.

kr., kreuzer (coin) Austria, Baden, Bavaria, Germany, Hungary, Wurttemberg.

krone, kronen (coin) Austria.

K.U.K. Imperial and Royal — Austria, Bosnia and Herzegovina.

K. WURTT Wurttemberg.

L

laid paper lines appear in vertical or horizontal directions. The wide-spread lines and the thin lines at right angles are the laid lines impressed in the paper substance.

land-post porto-marke Baden.

lat 100 santims. Coins of Latvia introduced in 1923.

LATVIJA, LATWIJA Latvia.

LIBAN, LIBANAISE Lebanon.

LIETUVA, LIETVOS Lithuania.

local stamps issues valid in a limited area like the U.S. postmasters' stamps used in cities, or the Confederate postmasters' stamps used during the early years of the U.S. Civil War. The Russian people issued locals called Zemstvos. Locals were not valid for postage from one country to another.

Losen   Sweden postage due stamps.

L'O.U.A. (part of Fr. insc.)   appears on stamps of the Republic of Guinea, May 25, 1973 meaning l'Organisation de l'Unite Africaine or in English: Organization of African Unity. The Organization established in May 1963 included Continental African States, Malagasy Republic (formerly Madagascar) and other islands surrounding Africa. (Courtesy of Republic of Guinea new stamp issue notice postmarked Sept. 3, 1973.)

LUXEMBURG   Luxembourg.

M

M   on stamps of Malta means mils introduced in 1972. 10 mils equal one cent. 100 cents equal 1 Malta pound.

MACAU or MACAV   Macao.

MAGYAR   Hungarian, Hungary.

MAGYARORSZAG   Hungary.

Maltese Cross   a design used in the first cancellation for British postage stamps in May 1840. The design is also incorporated in the postage stamps of Malta.

Maltese cross

mapka (coin) Russia, Finland, Serbia.

margins   the borders around most postage stamps where the perforations or roulettes are made. Margins around sheets or panes of stamps are known as marginal paper.

mark, markkaa (coin)   Finland.

MAROC   France — Offices in Morocco.

MARRUECOS   Spain — Offices in Morocco.

MBRETNIJA SHQIPTARE   Albania.

M.E.F.   overprinted on stamps of Great Britain — Offices in Africa.

MEJICO   Mexico.

meter postage stamps   impressions on envelopes or tapes replace adhesive postage stamps.

millimetre or millimeter   one thousandth of a metre. Philatelists use this metric unit to measure postage stamps. For example: the size of the Harding memorial U.S. stamps make a catalogue difference between eight cents and $7000 for used examples.

MOCAMBIQUE   Mozambique.

moiré   (Fr.) a pattern of lines overprinted or underprinted on postage stamps as a security measure.

MOROCCO AGENCIES   Great Britain — Offices in Morocco.

MOYEN CONGO   Middle Congo.

multicoloured   stamps printed in three or more colours by any printing method.

MX   a common short form of Maltese Cross describing the first cancellation on British postage stamps of 1840 and certain subsequent years. Often seen in dealers' advertisements.

N

NAPA Serbia.

NED. ANTILLEN Netherlands Antiles formerly Curaçao.

NEDERLAND Netherlands.

Netherlands postage due

NEZAVISNA DRZAVA HRVATSKA Croatia. Overprinted on stamps of Jugoslavia, 1941.

NOPTO MAPKA (insc.) Serbia postage due stamps.

NORGE Norway.

Norway official stamp

NOYTA (insc.) postage. Russia

numeral cancels early types showing various numerals that 1) indicate the original place where the stamps were cancelled or 2) in some U.S. post offices the numerals indicated the number of the cancelling device sometimes called a hammer owing to its shape like a tool.

Numeral cancellation

N.W. PACIFIC ISLANDS overprinted on stamps of Australia, North West Pacific Islands.

N.Z. New Zealand.

O

OAHAMAPKA Finland. On stamps in early issues

obliteration a cancel without details, just a variety of designs, numerals, bars or circles.

obsolescent the stamps that will be obsolete when new stamps arrive. The King George VI stamps were obsolescent when the King died. That is merely one example.

obsolete in stamp collecting, a stamp no longer in use after new issues replace them. For example: when King George VI of Great Britain died, all British, Colonial and Dominions postage stamps bearing his portrait became obsolete.

O.C.A.M. (insc.) Organisation Commune African Malgache and Mauricienne, Conference 1973. Appears on stamps of Mauritius with inscribed dates: 25 Avril (April) 6 Mai (May) 73 (1973).

OCEANIE French Oceania.

OFFENTLIG SAK (Insc.) Norway official stamps since 1926. Also: OFF SAK.

official stamps the kind made especially for use by government departments.

offisieel official, South-West Africa.

OG abbreviation for original gum on a stamp as it left the post office.

on covers refers to stamps on envelopes or other mail as it passed through the post.

OSTERREICH   Austria.

OSTERR-POST, OSTERREICHISCHE POST   Austria.

overprint   printing added to stamps after they were printed, but with no change in value. (See surcharge.)

P

Pacchi Postali   (insc.) on parcel post stamps of Italy and San Marino. Printed in two halves, one goes on the parcel and the other is a receipt for the customer. Used pairs are not available.

pair of stamps   two stamps joined either horizontally or vertically. Larger units less than a sheet or pane are called strips or blocks if they exceed three or more stamps from two or more horizontal rows.

pane   describes two types of postage stamp formats: 1) part of a sheet that may contain any number of panes of two or more. 2) Booklet postage comes in small panes from three to 25 or more stamps known as booklet panes.

pen, penni, pennias (coin)   Finland.

perforation gauge   a cardboard, plastic or metal device with markings to show the sizes of perforations, that is the number of holes in two centimetres. Often shortened to perf gauge.

PERSANE   Persia or Iran.

pesetas (coin)   with no country name, Spain.

pfennig   coins of Germany, Bavaria and Wurttemberg

pictorials   postage stamps with pictures of landscapes, oceans and skies but not portraits, fanciful designs or heraldic motifs.

pies (coin)   India.

PILIPINAS   Philippines under Japanese Occupation.

plate number block or plate block   four or more stamps with the marginal paper attached that bears the numbers of the printing plate used to produce those particular stamps.

P.N.G.   Papua New Guinea. On Dec. 5, 1973 Papua New Guinea issued 7-cent and 10-cent stamps to commemorate self-government of these former Australian Territories. The 1973 designs feature native carved heads from four regions of the territory.

porte de mar   Mexico.

POCZTA or POLSKA   Poland.

PORTEADO   Portugal.

porte franco   Peru, Portugal.

porto   on stamps bearing no country name — Austria.

postage and revenue   inscription on certain stamps mainly British and British colonial stamps to show they can be used for either postal or revenue service.

postage due   with denominations in pence or shillings — Great Britain or Australia.

postage due stamps   adhesive stamps or impressions struck on letters and other mail. The handstruck postage dues often have a word tax or taxe and the handwritten amount the receiver had to pay.

postas le nioc   Ireland (Eire).

poste aerieo or poste aerienne   on stamps with no country name — Persia.

postmarks   any marks struck on mail as it passes through post offices. Postal markings made by hand or machines. Vary from the earliest Bishop Marks of 1661 and following years in England. Hundreds if not thousands of different postmarks have been used in the past centuries.

POSTE VATICANE   Vatican City.

postzegel   with no country name given — Netherlands.

P.R.C. issues   People's Republic of China stamps of the communist republic. Stamps issued since Oct. 8, 1949.

provisional stamps   temporary or makeshift stamps for use until regular stamps replace them.

PTO. RICO, PUERTO RICO   (insc.) Stamps of Puerto Rico issued under Spanish dominion.

PYB or Pyb (coin) Russia or Finland.

Q

Qatar   Arab sheikdom on the Persian Gulf. Some of their stamps are rejected by the American Philatelic Society, because they are unnecessary. Junior Stamp Bugs beware.

Q.E. II   Queen Elizabeth the Second of Great Britain.

quartz lamp   an ultra violet lamp (black light) used by stamp collectors to detect tagged stamps or those printed on papers that glow under black light. Ultra violet light also reveals some repairs or removed pen and ink or manuscript cancels

quadrille   1) a type of watermark with squares or rectangles. 2) stamp album pages bearing small light squares as guides for mounting stamps.

Queensland   an Australian State in the northeastern part of Australia. Issued stamps from 1860 until 1907-12. Stamps of the Commonwealth of Australia used since 1913.

quetzal   sacred bird of Guatemala on many stamps of the country as the national emblem. Also name of the highest coin, one quetzal is equal to 100 centavos.

Q.V.   Queen Victoria of Great Britain.

R

rappen (coin)   Switzerland.

RARATONGA   one of the Cook Islands.

REICHSPOST   (insc.) on the stamps of Germany, mainly 1889-1900.

reis (coin)   with no country name given — Portugal

reprints   stamps printed from original plates after the stamps were obsolete. Usually made for stamp collectors. Austria and the United States reprinted certain stamps for exhibitions.

REPUB. FRANC or REPUBLIQUE FRANÇAISE   France or French Colonies.

Republik Maluku Selatan   (insc.) on labels reported to have been made with the hope of claiming certain parts of the Republic of Indonesia. Privately made labels had no postal use, hence they are not listed in Scott's Postage Stamp Catalogues.

R.F. (abbr.)   with no country name — France. Republic of France.

RHEINLAND-PFALZ   French occupation stamps for the Rhineland Palatinate (1947-9) area of Germany.

RIALTAR SEALDAC NA HEIREANN   Provisional Republic of Ireland overprinted on stamps of Great Britain — Eire or Irish Free State.

R.L.O.   Return Letter Office appeared on British redirected labels. The Inland Post Amendment Treasury Warrant, 1894, effective Jan. 1, 1895. No. 2 allowed all postal packets other than parcels to be redirected free of charge provided that the time rule was complied with.

rouletting   a method of making slits between postage stamps for easy separation. This process does not make holes in the paper.

rublis   coin of Latvia used 1918-23, divided into 100 kapeikas. Latvia introduced different coinage in 1923: 100 santims equal 1 lat.

running stag of Israel   David Remez, the first Minister of Transport and Communications of Israel in 1948, suggested the use of this symbol based on the biblical verse in 2 Samuel 2:18 King James version which reads in part, "and Asahel was as light of foot as a wild roe."

S

SAARE (ovpt.)   on stamps of Germany — Saar.

SAARGEBIET   Saar Territory — Saar.

SACHSEN   Saxony.

SAHARA ESPANOL or OCCIDENTAL   Spanish Western Sahara.

SAORSTAT EIREANN   Free State of Ireland overprinted on stamps of Great Britain — Irish Free State.

scar proof   a defaced proof sometimes with light hardly visible but sufficiently evident to destroy the proof and prevent it from being sold as a genuine postage stamp.

segna tassa or segnatasse   Italy, postage due.

semi-postal stamps   usually stamps with two denominations one for postage and the second for some predetermined charity or other project. They are often called charity stamps.

sen, sn (coins)   Japan.

se-tenant stamps   postage stamps of different values, designs, colours or with labels printed side by side in sheets, panes or souvenir sheets and even coils.

SHANGHAI   on U.S. stamps, United States Offices in China.

SHQIPNI, SHQIPNIJA, SHQIPONIES, SHQUIPENIA, SHQYPTARE   Albania.

skilling (coin)   Denmark, Norway.

SLESVIG   Schleswig-Holstein.

sld   (insc.) soldi, coin abbreviation printed on the stamps for use in the offices of Austria in the Turkish Empire. 100 soldi equal one florin.

SLOVENSKO   part of the inscription of 1918 stamps of Czechoslovakia on the right side. Left side reads CESKO.

S. MARINO   San Marino.

sobreporte   no country name Colombia. Stamps paid extra charges on mail to countries with no postal conventions with Colombia.

SOCIETE DES NATIONS   League of Nations, Switzerland, official stamps for the League.

soldi (coin)   Austria — Lombardy Venetia.

SOMALIA   Italian Somaliland.

SOUDAN   overprinted on stamps of Egypt — Sudan.

SOUDAN FRANÇAIS   French Sudan.

South Kasai   a part of one Congo province declared itself an autonomous state that issued stamps in 1961. Some were overprinted on stamps of Congo (ex-Belgian) stamps. Established nations did not recognize South Kasai as an independent state. (Courtesy *Scott Standard Postage Stamp Catalogue, Volume III.*)

space fillers   any stamp, forgery, poor quality or reprint, used to fill a space in a stamp album.

spandrels   corner ornaments that fill the spaces between oval or circular frames of the main design and the edges of stamps.

specimen stamps   usually overprinted or punched with the word SPECIMEN. Made for samples to be sent to the Universal Postal Union or for news items sent to philatelic writers in newspapers and stamp magazines.

split stamps   those cut into any portions other than halves to supply the stamps for the correct rates, especially during times of shortages of the required denominations. Not to be confused with bisected stamps.

stamps on stamps   a kind of postage stamp designs that feature one or more postage stamps as the central motif. (Some stamps have two motifs.) Scores of countries have used these designs to such an extent that entire collections of them may be formed.

stamp vending machine   a device made to eject postage stamps when coins are inserted. These machines contain roll postage (coils) or regular stamps in paper or cardboard covers.

S. THOME E PRINCIPE   St. Thomas and Prince Islands.

stothhkh (coin)   Bulgaria.

straight edge   a normally perforated stamp with one to three unperforated edges. Stamp collectors do not buy straight edge stamps as a general rule. Note the difference between these and coil stamps.

SUIDAFRIKA   Union of South Africa or South Africa.

SUIDWES AFRIKA or S.W.A.   South West Africa.

sul bollettino or sulla ricevuta   Italy, these stamps were also overprinted for some Italian Colonies. They are parcel post stamps.

Italy parcel post

SUOMI   Finland.

SURINAME   Surinam or Dutch Guiana.

surtax   the extra money people pay for charity or semi-postal stamps. The surtax most often is the smaller of two values on these stamps.

SVERIGE   Sweden.

S.W.A.   overprinted on stamps of South Africa — South-West Africa.

SWAZIELAND   Swaziland.

SYRIE, SYRIENNE   Syria.

T

tagged stamps   refers to postage stamps made for use in electronic mail sorting machines in large post offices in all parts of the world. (Tagging is the popular name for the process in Canada and the United States.) Some tagged stamps, mostly those in Great Britain, Canada and Japan, have bars. On certain stamps of South Africa the frames are printed with the luminescent chemicals for the similar purpose of speeding the handling of mail in post offices. Introduced in 1959 by Great Britain as experimental operations, the idea soon spread around the world to Germany in 1961, Canada and Denmark in 1962, and in the next year to the United States, Australia, the Netherlands and Switzerland. The U.S. Post Office issues postage stamps with an entire overprint of a luminescent chemical that is applied to the face of postage stamps after they were printed.

Takca   Bulgaria, Taxa de Plata   Romania, Takse or Taxe   Albania, inscriptions on postage due stamps of these countries.

TAXXA POSTALI   (insc.) appears on first decimal postage due stamps of Malta issued in 1973.

TCHAD   Chad. Became a separate French colony in 1920, and a republic in 1958.

T.C. POSTALARI   Turkey   (insc.) appears on some airmail stamps.

te betalen   Netherlands, Dutch Indies, Curaçao and Surinam; also preceded by a payer — Belgium. Postage due stamps.

telegrafos   Philippines.

TERRITORIOS (or TERRS.) ESPANOLES DEL GOLFO DE GUINEA   Spanish Guinea.

tête-bêche stamps   individual stamps or panes arranged upside down to each other.

THAILAND or THAI   Thailand or Siam.

tied to piece or cover   a stamp or stamps on the original paper cancelled partly on the stamps with the remaining part on the paper so that the entire cancel may be seen and understood. Bisects and split postage should be tied to a cover or at least a piece to prove their genuine use.

Timbre taxe   with numeral but no country name, French Colonies postage due stamps.

TJENESTE FRIMARKE   (insc.) on official stamps of Denmark, 1871 to 1924. Stamps have no country name.

toea   low value coins of Papua New Guinea introduced to replace the former cents. A new series of five stamps issued on April 21, 1975 illustrates both the toea and the kina that replaced the dollar. (See kina.)

TOGA   Tonga. Also known as the Friendly Islands in the Central Pacific. Gained fame for the Tin-Can mail from 1930 by letters with many chachets.

to pay   Great Britain, postage due stamps.

too late stamps and postmarks   indicate late delivery of mail to post offices after the mail had closed for the day. For an extra fee a person could send mail after hours.

TUNIS, TUNISIE   Tunisia.

TURKIYE, TURK POSTALARI   Turkey.

TUVALU   British Crown Colony formerly called the Ellice Islands that for over 80 years formed part of the colony of Gilbert and Ellice Islands. Tuvalu spreads over several hundred thousand square miles with the capital on the atoll of Funafuti. On Jan. 1, 1976 the first postage stamps were the current Gilbert and Ellice Islands stamps overprinted Tuvalu.

U

UAPCTBO   Bulgaria.

ultramar   beyond the sea with a year date, Cuba Porto Rico; with denominations in avos or reis — Macao, Guinea. Spelled Puerto Rico since May, 1932.

underprinting   printing on the back of stamps to provide security, describe each stamp or as Nicaragua did in 1911 surcharged revenue stamps on the back for postal use.

Universal Postal Union   1874-1949 (insc.) British commemorative stamps to mark the 75th anniversary of the U.P.U.

UNIVERSAL POSTAL UNION   Also known as the U.P.U. — a worldwide organization formed to regulate subjects regarding mail distribution and international postal difficulties such as postal rates, ocean mail, and the international exchange of mail. Montgomery Blair, the Postmaster General of the United States under President Lincoln, suggested a meeting of all countries that had diplomatic relations with the United States. A meeting that took place in 1863 in Paris resolved a set of the procedures for some future time. The War between the North and South in the United States caused a delay of nearly ten years in further activities. In September 1874 Dr. Heinrich von Stephan of Germany convened another conference at Bern in Switzerland. Delegates from 22 countries attended and eventually formed the General Postal Union. Three years later the organization changed the name to the Universal Postal Union.

V

VAN DIEMEN'S LAND   the original name of Tasmania.

varieties   stamps that have some different, individual character in their production such as ink smears, blemish or microscopic ink dots, faulty perforations of any kind. Any exposure of the stamps to light or gases that change the colour may produce another kind of variety. Postage stamps printed in identical designs and values by flat plates or curved plates from rotary presses differ in size in one direction. They are also varieties, not errors. The Harding memorial U.S. stamps are examples of the same stamps from flat and curved plates. Lithographed stamps often contain small specks that are varieties. Machines and other equipment create varieties; human beings make errors.

V.A.T.   Value Added Tax, a form of British taxation that began on April 1, 1973. Virtually everything in Britain sold at retail prices bears the tax, excepting new or used books. Even postage stamps for collections are taxed under this law.

VATICANE   Vatican City.

vom empfanger einzuziehen   (insc.) postage due, Danzig, a former free city in Northern Europe.

W

war tax stamps   special postage stamps with a surtax for extra revenue for the countries that issued them, mainly during the First World War in Canada and some British colonies. Stamps were inscribed or overprinted. Spain issued war tax stamps 1874 to 1898.

watermarks   designs of scores of subjects: letters, numerals, crowns, anchors, animal heads, fruit, and others seen by holding stamps in front of light. Watermarks are produced by raised impressions on the dandy roll of a paper machine. (See dandy roll and laid paper lines.)

WIPA   Austria. On stamps and souvenir sheet issued for the International Stamp Exhibition in June, 1933

wn (coin)   Korea.

X

ΧΑΡΤΟΣΗΜΟΝ   Greece.

X cancel   huge cancellation on high value King George VI stamps of India to deface the Kings portrait, mainly 1937-48 issue

X on stamp labels   known as the St. Andrew's Cross was used to fill empty spaces in sheets of stamps to prevent forgers from getting genuine paper for counterfeits. These should not be separated from the adjacent postage stamps.

XMAS 1898   (insc.) on Canadian stamps of 1898 showing a map of the world with some British colonies and dominions printed in red. These stamps were issued for first-day use overseas on Christmas Day, 1898 to introduce the penny postage rate to the places appearing in red on the stamps.

x-ray philately   studious attempts to study postage stamps and examine them by an x-ray machine. Repairs and faked two-colour stamps with inverted centres or frames show clearly on the x-ray plates. Black light does a similar job.

Y

yacht keytypes   German colonial stamps feature Kaiser Wilhelm Hohenzollern's yacht sailing on a choppy sea. Spaces on the stamps bear the colonial names and the denominations for each colony.

yen   Japanese coin equal to 100 sen.

Yvert et Tellier catalogues   the leading French postage stamp catalogues.

Z

Zaire   Republic in Central Africa, formerly Congo Democratic Republic, changed its name in November, 1971. Issued first stamps in December, 1971.

Zambia   former British protectorate of Northern Rhodesia, became an independent republic in October, 1964. Changed its name to Zambia and issued three stamps to mark the event on Oct. 24.

Zambezia   a former district of Mozambique province of Portuguese East Africa. Issued

Portuguese colonial (Keytype) stamps 1894-1917. (See stamp catalogues.)

Zanzibar   former British Protectorate, a group of islands about 20 miles off the coast of East Africa in the Indian Ocean. Became independent on Dec.10,1963. Zanzibar united with Tanganyika in April, 1964 to form the United Republic of Tanganyika and Zanzibar. Name changed to Tanzania. (See stamp catalogues.)

ZAR or Z. AFR REP   (ovpt. and inscs.) Africaans words for Zuid Afrikaansche Republiek on stamps of the South African Republic, listed in catalogues under Transvaal.

Zeitung   German for journal or newspaper, hence newspaper stamps. Examples: Austria 1851-1922.

Zeppelin stamps   postage stamps issued to prepay airmail charges on Zeppelins and other rigid airships mainly German, British and United States naval ships, the Macon and Akron. Stamps that illustrate Zeppelins are often called Zeppelin stamps.

zig zag roulette   (French percé en pointes) a type of roulette with sharp pointed teeth resembling fine perforations.

J
383   Patrick
Pat

The Stamp bug: An Illustrated
introduction to stamp collecting